QUEERSAPIEN

Praise for the book

'*Queersapien* is a coming-of-age book. It doesn't sell promises of instant solutions with a side order of rose-tinted glasses; rather it is a quiet path to answers, hope and a sort of goosebumpy upliftment. In a time of growing intolerance, it discovers the nooks and crannies of coexistence within each of us. It is a book about the billion-hued rainbow we call real life.'

—**Seema Anand**, mythologist, storyteller and author

'Man is born free, Rousseau reminded us, but is everywhere in chains. The chains are social, cultural, political, economic, institutional. None are more damaging to the self than the chains that stunt our imagination, our mind, our ideas of right and wrong, indeed our sense of self. Sharif D. Rangnekar brings to us the lived experience of liberation from such chains. A compelling read.'

—**Dr Sanjaya Baru**, economist and writer

'A moving personal testament to the fact that queerness resides not just in the individual but also in her geography. This book is more than an autobiography; it is an attempt to explore the intimate relation between the public act of love and private act of self-exploration.'

—**Saurabh Kirpal**, Senior Advocate of the Supreme Court and author of *Sex and The Supreme Court*

'Nature doesn't discriminate and neither should we. Under the sky, below the clouds, bathed in moonlight or sunshine or, indeed, knee-deep in snow, we are equal. And if our quirks make us interesting and human, these must be appreciated in each of us, whatever one's faith, creed or sexuality might be. I've always agonized over how much or how little it takes to be kind and civil to one another; how impossible, after all, can this be. Sharif's account, I'm hoping, will only make it easier to cross the bridge. Towards understanding.'

—**Tanuja Chandra**, filmmaker and writer

'Never have I read a book that captures the multiple geographies of the heart and traverses both inner and outer worlds so effortlessly. If Sharif's debut book was a revelation, this follow-up is a revolution—both a reflection of times gone by as well as a call to action to create a better world in which we can all thrive.'

—**Parmesh Shahani**, author of *Queeristan: LGBTQ Inclusion in the Indian Workplace*

'As a parent of a queer child, I know what queerness means, but Sharif's book reinvents, expands and amplifies what I might understand about queerness. This book attempts to comprehend queerness by holding it up to the light and looking at it from various sociopolitical lenses, diving into historical moments of our nation as well as his personal experiences. A must read!'

—**Aruna Desai**, co-founder, Sweekar, The Rainbow Parents

'*Queersapien* carried me along its deceptively effortless flow of writing—past some roads that were familiar, other signposts that hinted at stories still to be told—all captivated me till the last page. What moved me was the interweave of his personal journey that traverses peril, loss and deep empathy to finally come home to love, freedom, identity and dignity. This in a society where family, gender roles, religion, caste and class intersect, sometimes randomly, at other times, the dictates of norms compelling one to 'fit in'. But, interestingly, this book resists a thematic box, much like queerness: it is a quiet evolution of the self, in tandem with an emerging community, a nation and its people.'

—**Maya Sharma**, author, feminist grassroots activist and co-founder, Vikalp

'At a time when gayness is rapidly becoming a brand, a liberal fashion accessory with rainbow emojis, Sharif D. Rangnekar queers the pitch. With a lens that's personal and probing, he frees queerness from the straitjackets of both victimhood and coolness as he explores the ideas of freedom, diversity, minority, inclusion and, yes, love, in India, issues that should resonate far beyond the LGBTQ+ discourse.'

—**Sandip Roy**, author of *Don't Let Him Know*

'Insightful, evocative, bold, unique and queer to the core, Sharif D. Rangnekar's groundbreaking book tears into all that ails our society, and lends new meaning to queerness. *Queersapien* is a must-read for anyone who believes in equality, freedom and justice.'

—**Saif Mahmood,** Senior Advocate of the Supreme Court and author of *Beloved Delhi: A Mughal City and Her Greatest Poets*

'Despite being a trans woman myself, I found this book to be flooded with fascinating insights about the queer world that were nothing short of epiphanies for me. What is striking about *Queersapien* is that it manages to be two poignant books in one. It handholds you into discovering the boundless queerness in the world around you while also taking you into the boundless world inside a queer person. Sharif's prose has a surprising yet tender fluidity to it, much like the view of humankind he opens your eyes to. My favourite bits of this remarkable book are the writer's beautiful relationship with his quietly magnificent mother, and his perception of that queerly universal ache called love.'

—**Gazal Dhaliwal**, screenwriter

Also by the author

Straight to Normal: My Life as a Gay Man
Realizing Brand India: The Changing Face Of Contemporary India

QUEERSAPIEN

SHARIF D. RANGNEKAR

RUPA

Published by
Rupa Publications India Pvt. Ltd 2022
7/16, Ansari Road, Daryaganj
New Delhi 110002

Sales centres:
Allahabad Bengaluru Chennai
Hyderabad Jaipur Kathmandu
Kolkata Mumbai

P-ISBN: 978-93-5520-810-1
E-ISBN: 978-93-5520-811-8

First impression 2022

10 9 8 7 6 5 4 3 2 1

Printed in India

For

My late father, Dr D.K. Rangnekar,
mother, Veena Rangnekar,
and eldest brother, Dilip Rangnekar,
late brother, Dr Dwijen D. Rangnekar.
All my family living in different parts of the world.

All those who identify as queer, and those who have and continue to fight for our rights, the people lost along the way and the ones who are struggling to 'come out' to themselves. All those who don't wish to conform or 'fit in', no matter what their gender or sexuality.

All those who loved me and gave me an opportunity to love back.
The love of my life, Roshan Wosti, a person who has helped me realize that there is no age for love, that I can still open my heart to love and love madly!

I was so much older then,
I'm younger than that now

—Bob Dylan

CONTENTS

PREFACE

THE QUEERSAPIEN I AM, WE CAN BE

Being queer isn't about one thing. Nor is queerness. Queerness exists outside the box. It is defined by the indefinite, the expanse, the width and length, the roundness of the Earth. It is coloured by colours. It isn't one colour. So, seeing things from a queer standpoint or lens or view isn't about one idea or thought either. It is as diverse as it can get. It recognizes that there are many ways to live and as many ways to die.

Queerness intersects with what is called the mainstream and yet may seem alternate to it. It intersects with every disability—the hurdles and divisiveness of class, caste, religion, creed and colour. It is human, and hence, like heterosexuals, it needs love as it needs air, water, food and shelter. It needs family, but it is wise enough to know that blood isn't necessarily thicker than water, that there are choices to exercise. That everything acquired at birth, be it family, caste, class or religion, are veneers and boxes that can often put constraints on liberties or deny them altogether. Queerness recognizes, what Kavita Krishnan says is the contradiction at the heart of Indian families, that bandhan means both bond and bondage.[1]

This doesn't mean that being queer is being oblivious of the fact that freedom isn't absolute or queerness isn't absolute. It acknowledges that both being queer and being free are journeys. It is about change and evolution. It knows, just like Bob Dylan says, 'No one is free, even birds are caged to the sky'. But between land, the seas and sky, there is enough space for freedom to be experienced and expressed.

To be queer is about roles, chosen ones. Queerness would want to free men of the tireless expectation of being a breadwinner and provider. It would wish for women to actualize themselves through what they choose. In a way, to be queer is to remove the hoods from manhood and womanhood, and let honesty and integrity prevail. It is to recognize each individual's desires and pleasures as possibilities, without ignoring or celebrating the biological roles of reproduction attached to a woman and her womb, and a man and his semen.

Queerness doesn't put a premium on virginity. It doesn't see virginity as purity. It knows that everything is part of evolution, part of fucks and fuckups. It is the understanding that there are starting points and then miles to cover. Queerness is about

---

[1]Krishnan, Kavita, *Fearless Freedom*, Penguin Random House, 2020.

living before dying and being born again and again to relish the freshness of innocence and curiosity.

To be queer isn't to demean any faith, be it the faith in religion, gurus, science, education and political ideologies. It knows that when weaponized, one religion can hate another; that even the progress of science can result in wars. It knows that one sort of education can mock another, that gurus can do the same, so do those on the Left and Right of the political divide.

In all the diversity queerness sees, it has a high regard for the many delightful facets of nature. For instance, it knows water is water. Yet, it also sees water as the sea, the rain, snow, ice, puddles, lakes, rivers, rivulets, hail, steam, dew, waterfalls, floods and every other avatar it has. Queerness acknowledges biodiversity in trees, forests and woods; there isn't one like the other, not one flower like the other. It is conscious of the fact that if left free, trees are more rooted and stronger. That even creepers find their way up a tree to get some sun.

Similarly, to be queer is to know that the air can be cool and hot, that it can be a typhoon, a tornado and can be so still, it goes unnoticed. It absorbs the importance of the earth, the soil, the undulations, the hills and mountains. It knows that with all its strength, it can crumble, and in that collapse, there is rejuvenation.

A queer mind sees all of this and sees itself in the variety nature offers. And hence, it knows that if the blinkers we wear to view life with are removed, we'd all know that there isn't one kind of being. There isn't one way to live. There isn't one kind of food. There isn't a single form to clothing, education and wisdom. Nor is there one version of history and culture or one kind of war. There isn't a singular structure to a family, a union or one way to love. Queerness, therefore, instinctively knows there isn't one sexuality. There is LGBTQIA+.

Some may argue that this is a simplistic way of looking at life. Sure, but why complicate it?

If some ask for scientific evidence, I will say there is enough of that already in the public domain. I'd refer to various scientific and medical bodies, including the Indian Psychiatric Society, which has more than once stated that the LGBTQIA+ community is sane, legitimate and 'normal'.[2] I'd present what Dr Hansaji Yogendra of the Yoga Institute (founded in 1918) said in a video released in 2021—that sexual orientation is 'inborn' and choiceless.[2] I would refer to court orders and comments. I would say dig into history, read the Mahabharata, the Kama Sutra, or find out about the roles Lord Vishnu played. Queerness, however, is not about turning back time; it is about turning things around.

Of course, we can all head to conferences and roundtables debating this endlessly. We can expand the discussion into every aspect of life, heterosexuality, too, and queer animals as well. And that isn't a bad option at all, as to question the normative ideas and perspectives is queer too. To be queer is to prefer democracy and to uphold its tenets.

So, what is normal? All of this. There isn't one normal if

---

[2]'Have you accepted your sexual orientation completely? | Dr. Hansaji Yogendra', YouTube, https://youtu.be/q8ZPRCxO440. Accessed on 20 September 2022.

we take it out of the hands of limited societal imaginations, rules and norms, and just let people be.

Like nature, there will be natural calamities. There is good and bad. There are cool and hot times. There is turbulence, earthquakes and storms. There is loss and gain. As queer folks, we accept this, and to be honest to ourselves, we accept our vulnerabilities to come to the point where we know we have nothing to lose but darkness. That behind darkness, there is beauty, expression, innovation and art.

Art, as you'd know, in its most honest and raw form, emerges from a space of free thinking, without any binaries, restrictions, constructs or labels. It is about the recognition that just like nature, we are all beautiful, that beauty doesn't need validation or an external description. As John Lennon said: 'When you do something beautiful and nobody notices, do not be sad. For the sun, every morning is a beautiful spectacle and yet most of the audience still sleeps.'

In multiple ways, being queer is about being both alone and part of a marketplace and society. It is about meditation, the ability to shut out the audience, the judgements, the norms and structured moralities. It is about values. It is about valuing the self. It is to do with self-awareness and self-realization. It is about seeing oneself in others. It is what millennials call self-love. It is about love. But as Lennon said (and I quote him again): 'We need to learn to love ourselves first, in all our glory and our imperfections. If we cannot love ourselves, we cannot fully open to our ability to love others or our potential to create.'

To get to the sense that you have nothing to lose, however, isn't easy. Not in a world where nature itself seems irrelevant. Not in a world where political correctness is a benchmark even if it hides the truth. Not in a world where systems, processes and livelihood takes over one's mind, space and life. Not in a world that packages relationships and love with prescribed formulas, where love itself has become a commodity, not an emotion that needs time to grow and grow with.

As queer people, in all the liberation we can be, and the freedom we can open the world to, we still have to use labels. We need that sense of belonging. Labels and identities tell us, as it told me when I identified as gay, that there are others like us or myself, that we are not alone. In some ways, it is like being a non-resident Indian (NRI) in a foreign land, creating a club to feel connected with 'your people', countering the alienation felt or experienced in a nation that isn't yours. Like groups of freedom fighters and mutineers wanting to hold on to these identities and tags to distinguish themselves from their rulers and other complying citizens.

As a result, we have had to create our own little world in the midst of the larger one through non-governmental organizations (NGOs), community groups, online and offline, bars and cafes, queer affirmative healthcare centres, the Pride March and more. We have had to create and nurture a queer culture for self-actualization—supporting each other and finding love. And our flag, another symbol of Pride, is much like any other flag that is associated with or identifies with a nation, state and its people, just that we have to hoist it across the world so that our marginalized folks know where they'd be safe and welcomed.

Queerness, as you'd probably guess, calls for strength—to make it through thick and thin, to be odd and use that oddity as a force in itself. It is a strife that we have to go through. It is about the winds that destroy us and the winds beneath our wings.

I would agree we aren't normal, as we aren't obsessed with the status quo. We are constructive, but we don't wish to build templates and fixtures that are almost immovable. We like boxes to pack things in, but that's not where we wish to live or exist. We'd hang our clothes in a closet, but that's not a place for us to hang in.

If you think along the same lines about life, the personal and the political, then you are amongst those who are queering the narratives or wishing to do so. And if you think it is natural to question, to seek change, to work towards it and to add to a debate, a perspective of unseen and unheard lenses that aren't of the typical heterosexual males, then you are queering the world too.

Of course, we'd like to hold on to our identity, our labels, for the reasons given above. But we'd never shut the door on allies and friends. Being queer is a belief in camaraderie irrespective of differences, the given roles we have or the one's we adopt and choose to have.

But, I know, through my journey in life and experiences with love, family, politics, media, religions, cultures, nations and people, queering is a process. It is a constant effort to retain one's sense of self. And since freedom and queerness aren't absolute or constant, nor is any norm, as that defies nature's greatness to change, to have different seasons that are normal to some and not normal to all.

What I see and leave you with is not just this book. It is the thought that the opposite of order isn't disorder, it is diversity. And if you can include this thought in your consciousness, we'd all stand a chance to partake and share this beautiful world, its nature and our ability to give and receive love!

The world, after all, is queer, if you have enough curiosity to see it that way!

ONE
JUDGEMENT

'History owes an apology to the members of this community and their families, for the delay in providing redressal for the ignominy and ostracism that they have suffered through the centuries…'[1]

In this single sentence, the junior-most and only female judge, Indu Malhotra, in her written order reading down Section 377 decriminalizing 'gay sex' on 6 September 2018, expressed a regret and the reality of what we, the LGBTQIA+ community, have been through, trying to eke out a life bereft of dignity in the eyes of society. It seemed she understood what it was to be gay in India, how it was to live a life that wasn't

[1]'History Owes Apology to LGBT Community and Kin: Justice Indu Malhotra', *The Economic Times*, 6 September 2018, https://tinyurl.com/bdz7yyc2. Accessed on 20 September 2022.

full, where being oneself was a challenge and achievement, where to find a partner to love and be loved by was almost unattainable and a privilege.

For most of my life as a gay man I had been a criminal. Every time I slept with someone or indulged in sex against 'the order of nature', as Section 377 of the Indian Penal Code stated, I was guilty of acting against the law and could be arrested. Of course, the police had to literally catch me in the act to arrest me, which, fortunately, never happened. Across large parts of India, however, the police used the law to harass the community and, at times, even our well-wishers.

We grew up being called 'homo', 'fag-head', 'half a man', 'retard', 'weird', 'meetha' and God knows what else! We saw hate in the eyes of the uninformed homophobes. We saw interpretations of religion and customs being thrown at us as watertight norms, where we had no place or status. This, even if we were devoted to our gods, believing, as some did, that we are their creation.

We were repeatedly told about binaries and the stiff structures of a family—what it is to be part of it, and how gender and sexual orientation can't be distinct from each other—where fluidity was a flood of fear for the patriarchs who ruled a home, a family and society. We learnt that violence was almost always fine in a family, even if a parent beat up their child black and blue. The 'man' at home, as it were, could beat everyone else in that unit, since masculinity, the male ego, the muscle power, the bruteness that can come with it, had been legitimized over the years by society. So, it had become a norm, a practice accepted every day with the common refrain—*aisa hi hota hain* (this is how it is).

There is more to gain from an understanding of, for example, why it was important to stay silent when a crime was committed against you in a family set-up. That silence was aimed to maintain peace and a status quo, not to disturb the structure of a 'loving' family and not to become part of the gossip in society. Those who suffered, the victims of violence and the silence that followed, had to deal with mental torture, depression and, perhaps, the deep desire to end their lives. But that was their lot.

Fondness, respect, dignity and love were a privilege for a few who either had family support or chose their family from amongst friends. There were other lucky ones who were economically independent, making choices of their own, running away from India, finding a foreign partner to love and live with. Some, as history knows, even if not recorded in the media or elsewhere, gave up their lives, battling violence and a dehumanized existence.

As luck would have it, I had an expanding family of support and a large number of friends who cared. Still, I spent most of my life building courage to be myself, validate and fortify my existence, finally coming to a point where my queerness and I didn't require any public ratification or certificate. I was 50 by then!

The time spent and the life gone was so tedious, nerve-wracking and filled with mental ups and downs that I was left with no time to invest in love or a companionship in its truest form. This, of course, wasn't unique to me. A whole bunch of people from my time had struggled to find love and to hold on to it in a world where our queer lives had been limited, largely, to the four walls of a home and a bedroom.

No wonder then, when the over-17-year-old legal battle to have Section 377 read down culminated with the decriminalization of 'gay sex' in September 2018, I felt nothing but a sense of relief. I didn't feel the elation that many of the younger generation present outside the apex court displayed. I couldn't relate to the headlines of love and triumph and the generous use of the word 'freedom'.

On that milestone day, sections of the press quoted and praised Judge Malhotra's comment that history owed us an apology. Yet, strangely, they didn't seem to try and understand what she meant or inferred. She clearly established the fact that, for centuries, we have been wronged, that society has been homophobic, hateful and guilty of not treating us equally and that today we should be considered equal citizens.

If we dig deeper, just slightly, we'd all know that society and history is not made by a single person or institution; it is always a combination of influencers and influences. In this case, the guilt of wrongdoing, in all honesty, sits with the media, politicians, film stars, celebrities, educators, doctors, lawmakers, leaders of religious groups, yoga and spiritual gurus, just to name a few.

I wept for hours the day after the order, as did many others. These weren't tears of joy over the triumph in the Supreme Court but over Judge Malhotra's candid admission of our 'trials' and lived history—that someone acknowledged our truth. It was also the realization that I was still single. For years, I had held myself responsible for my failed relationships, not examining sufficiently that there was more to it than just me and my actions or those of my boyfriends. I used to compare my success (as the world saw it) in my professional life with my private, emotional one. I touched so many highs in my career, but there were many more lows when it came to love and companionship.

I, of course, didn't have wisdom of hindsight to know that the comparison itself was flawed and unfair. I worked in journalism and public relations, which, by and large, had a stated path, the daily grind and an ecosystem of certainty, accepted by society. Queer love was politically excluded, morally unacceptable and socially much hated.

For days and weeks following the verdict, this truth, our history and the lives of a large number of LGBTQIA+ folks was quietly erased, unintentionally, I hope. In fact, within hours of the reading down of Section 377, the order was turned into a declaration of love and freedom. What took centre stage was an emotive set of hashtags, heart-shaped emojis and headlines, such as 'love is love' and 'pure love', and a pronouncement of sorts by powerful sections of the media that we were free now!

This hyperbolic disproportionate representation of the judgement was reminiscent of yellow journalism. I remember when India emerged as the third-largest economy in the world (in terms of purchasing power parity), the media splashed it across the front page, ignoring the fact that close to or over

90 per cent of the population was not part of 'that' economy. Those who weren't included were disenfranchised, poor and mostly voiceless and under-represented!

Similarly, in the case of queer rights and the movement, only a miniscule number of Indians could celebrate 'pure love', 'love is love' and love itself, as it was a privilege not available or accessible to most. After all, being Indian, we carried the same caste and class system that society had built a system of social mobility.

As Maya Sharma, a feminist grassroots activist based in Vadodara, told me, 'The order will make it easier for us to roll out multiple healthcare and educational programmes in smaller towns and villages specific to the gay community. The police and society had used this law for moral policing, creating hurdles. *Pyaar aur ye sab door ki baat hain. Logo ka bachpan, unki suraksha sarvshreshtha hain* (forget about love right now. People's childhoods, their safety is of utmost importance).'

Importantly, if we take a rational and factual view of the September 6 judgement, it allows us to explore our sexuality through consensual sex, which would obviously happen in a private place. We have absolutely no other right that gives us dignity and equality in public, once we are out of our rooms. We will not be protected against hate crimes, including the common form of bullying in schools and colleges. We can be discriminated against at hospitals, educational institutions, workplaces and at home. Some of us, even today, over three years after the order and a Chennai High Court verdict outlawing conversion therapy, are being dragged by parents to doctors for shock treatment and hormonal medication so that their child 'returns' to being heterosexual.

While sections of influencers, including some in the press, believe the next steps for us are marriage and the fostering of relationships, they ignore the fact that to get to the point of self-determined partnerships, we need a strong foundation built around laws that protect us. We need allies who advocate for equal rights and a media that is truly inclusive and interested in our lives, with backstories of trials and tribulations, not just a 'massive' win.

Yet, the order was undeniably a significant one, as it led to an opening of discussions, dialogues, views and counterviews. It would be unfair to take away the joy of many a queer person who felt validated on the day of the judgement. It was a coming out moment for some, a time when they could claim a space in society and probably even at home. Some of the young had a chance to stand outside the apex court and kiss their partner—a person they met in college, through common friends or in a queer and gender group that several universities are now open to.

Many called their homes and revealed their sexuality to their families. In some cases, they took a step further by publicly recognizing their lovers or same-sex partners. Why wouldn't they—they weren't criminals any longer.

A little over three weeks after the famous order, I held a small dinner at home to thank Anjali Gopalan of Naz Foundation for all the efforts she had taken fighting for our rights from 2001, moving the Delhi High Court on Section 377. As usual, she was uncomfortable being central to the celebration that evening but opened up about the journey and how it had started.

She used to spend three to four hours of a day counselling mostly gay men. 'I met many who were being forced into marriages with women,' she said. In several cases, the parents were aware of their son's sexuality, and still, 'they insisted that their son could use his spare time to meet other men'. While that itself is absurd, unthinkable and reflective of male privilege in homes, 'not once did these parents consider what the women would go through,' said Anjali, with a frown crossing her forehead.

She recounted an even more worrisome situation. 'One day, a boy walked into our Naz office. He told us "I am being given shock treatment," she revealed. His parents, with the help of some doctors, were trying to 'convert' him from homosexuality to heterosexuality. And this was happening at a major hospital in South Delhi. This was the moment that Naz Foundation went to the National Human Rights Commission (NHRC) to bring the practice of conversion therapy and its risks to their notice. Their response was purely legal: it [men having sex with men] was a criminal activity.

With no option in hand, Anjali realized that there was an urgency to have Section 377 read down, which is when she turned to the noted lawyer Anand Grover and the Lawyer's Collective to move the courts.

This was 2001. Two decades later, boys and girls are still being forced into arranged marriages. If they protest and question their parents, they're locked in their rooms, thrashed into silence and submission, and are even forced into heterosexual sex, which amounts to rape. 'And parents can do this legally, as there are not enough laws to protect so many young LGBTQIA+ people. There are only a handful who can turn to courts to seek protection, if they are adults,' said Anjali in a very exasperated manner, knowing full well that even if there are laws, social stigma is enough to puncture anyone's dignity.

As she cut the 'thank you' truffle cake with a rainbow-coloured topping, she said there was a lot to do, as we needed to 'protect future generations so that children can build a more certain life for themselves'. True she was.

Months after Section 377 was read down, we lost a fashion stylist from Meghalaya; he ended his life fed up of the hate society inflicted on him. In 2019, a lesbian was tied up to a tree and beaten up in Madhya Pradesh. A schoolgoing boy in Chennai died of suicide after being bullied repeatedly by classmates for being gay and 'different'. Anjana Harish, a 21-year-old from Kerala, who identified as bisexual, went through the horror of 'conversion therapy', being kept in a cell for three weeks. She was later found hanging from a tree in Goa. Early in 2020, before the Covid-19 lockdown, a gay student of Indian Institute of Technology (IIT) Roorkee ended his life, indicating how even premier institutes are not necessarily safe enough for homosexuals. More recently, Arvey Malhotra, a student of Delhi Public School, Faridabad, left us, suffering at the hands of bullies who mocked at him for being 'feminine'. 'This is just the tip of the iceberg', said an official working with Humsafar Trust, 'suicides are on the rise across the rainbow spectrum' ever since the verdict. 'They (society) think we are free and now want to push us back', he said firmly.

Present at the dinner in honour of Anjali were a mix of queer people, including the editor of *Gaylaxy Magazine*, Sukhdeep Singh; Maisnam Arnapal, who taught English at the University of Delhi; Mr Gay India 2016, Anwesh Sahoo; besides some close friends and relatives. Sukhdeep, a techie by profession, had set up *Gaylaxy Magazine* over a decade ago, as he couldn't find any significant resource online for queer people when he came out. Anwesh was not just a pageant winner, he had emerged to be a voice for the community, a belly dancer and an admired graphic artist. Maisnam had chosen to keep a low profile, being an educator and belonging to a culture that he feared would not accept his sexuality.

Chatting away on the patio just outside the dining area, Anwesh told me that while his public profile was chirpy, social and 'queerly gorgeous', nothing was easy, not even living where he resided in Delhi. He had to take off his high-heeled shoes, 'usually worn by women', and replace them with keds before getting in to an auto, knowing full well he risked being harassed and violently attacked. 'I was bullied at school,' and even after Section 377 was read down, 'my parents were still unaware of what it is to be queer and what it is to have a life in a country such as ours,' he said in a dismissive manner, having learnt to make it on his own.

The option to leave India was on his mind. 'I hope work takes me there. Or I find a partner,' Anwesh exclaimed. 'I would prefer to live in Europe, the US or Canada,' he said.

Maisnam was working away to get admission into a university in a gay-friendly country for his PhD on queer lives and literature. 'If things work out, I would rather live outside India. It would be freer, easier to pursue my work and meet the desire to have a partner,' he told me in a matter-of-fact manner.

Sukhdeep was the odd one out or just slightly uncertain at this point, given his commitment to the e-magazine and the queer movement. He was also very close to his family and wondered 'if turbaned men like me would be well-received in other parts of the world'. Still, he was waiting to hear from different universities on his plans to pursue journalism and gender representation in the media.

By now, I knew artists, poets, scholars, dancers, lawyers, filmmakers, doctors, bankers and entrepreneurs who had not just moved out of their 'family' homes but had packed up and left the country with no desire to live in India or to return to their country of origin. This trend, as I saw it, had not ebbed even after a long period of two decades since I first came out in 1999. Gay men either came under pressure and got married or left their homes in small towns to find shelter and safety in larger urban cities. They either died of suicide or found a ticket out of India.

'You'd probably go to Thailand, wouldn't you?' asked Anwesh that night, knowing I was a rice queen—a person who fancied the Mongolian look. My answer wasn't definitive, in that I still wanted to fight, I carried hope and had to consider what my mother wanted, as she had always thought of my likes and dislikes, not just as a mother but as a friend too.

My family, though, was deeply concerned and keen that I found a partner, someone who would see me through my old age, if I got to an 'old' age. They were also aware that I loved Thailand and was enamoured by Thai culture and neighbouring countries such as Laos, Cambodia and the Philippines. My mother told me often, 'If that is what you want, go for it.' From relatives to friends, everyone wanted what was best for me, with a rider that they'd visit me wherever I lived.

The truth is, moving to Thailand had always been my Plan B. It was something for the future. I was almost convinced that Delhi would continue to disillusion me with what it had to offer, and certain that the dream of a safe society and a partner to live with was in the calms of Thailand. After all, it was in that kingdom I first experienced what it meant to be free as a gay man.

Why, then, would I not want to live there?

TWO

BANGKOK

It was 9 July 2004 when I made my first visit to Thailand, touching down at Bangkok's Don Muang Airport, a buzzing airport even at six in the morning. At that time, Bangkok was a key connection into other parts of Southeast Asia, East Asia and Asia Pacific. It was a city that most tourists didn't mind spending a night or two in on their way to their final destination. No wonder the old airport boasted of reportedly over 30 million passengers getting in and out of it, where cafés, restaurants, spas and stores were open 24 hours.

I was unsure what to expect of the city or Pattaya, which I was to visit too. All I knew was the popular 'selling points' of shopping, an active nightlife, sex and, for people like me, gay places. I had no priorities or a list of things to do, see or shop. All I was aware of was my desperation to get out of Delhi, to stretch my arms and feel free. And to, hopefully, find love, as all my efforts so far had come to naught.

What drew my attention and left me most pleased on landing and walking through the airport were the local Thai men I saw immediately on arrival. They were lithe and good-looking men, smiling the moment you spotted them, pushing baggage carts and wheelchairs, at information desks, stores; some just standing by gazing at nothing, probably waiting for their shift to end or start.

There were a lot of women at work, an absolute surprise to me. They were there as immigration officers, sweepers, spa managers, serving food at a café, manning retail stores and doing whatever other jobs men were doing. This, to me, was an indication of how safe the city was for them and how normal it was for women to work and earn a living.

The drive from the airport to the city revealed how modernized Bangkok was with its elevated roads, expressways crisscrossing through the city and its Manhattan-like skyline. Once we got off the multilevel eight-lane roads, I saw the real Bangkok—busy, slower-moving traffic, pavements with hawkers and a spirit of liveliness even at breakfast time.

Knowing that this was my first trip to Bangkok, the taxi driver asked, 'Is India like this? Tall buildings, like America?' I said no but talked about Mumbai and its beautiful Marine Drive, from where you could see Malabar Hill and the several buildings jutting out of the green. In my view, the two cities had a similar spirit and energy. Mumbai was just a terribly poor distant cousin, given its fragile infrastructure, spread of shanty towns and apparent economic inequalities. Delhi had broad roads, was far greener than Mumbai and Bangkok but had a damp spirit, if any, I thought.

The Thai capital was heavily influenced by the United States (US). This was due to its political affiliations and the consequent impact of Hollywood, American media and tourists. Yet, the city offered a lot more beyond the American, as it remained rooted in tradition, respect for Buddha and the King, and a pride in its arts, culture and food. So, if you found a wide variety of international brands in shopping malls and street stores, local brands had their place too. If there were burger, doughnut and pizza chains, Thai, Japanese and Korean food outlets were also in abundance. And as the driver told me, there were a lot of Indian restaurants close to the hotel I was to stay at. Indian food, of course, was least of my interest.

The taxi driver did take me by surprise when he asked, 'You like lady, pomp, pomp?' It was only when he used his fist, indicating a certain kind of sexual thrust, did I gather that 'pomp, pomp' meant sex. I just smiled and said, 'No sex for me.' He looked surprised and disappointed. I wondered why. It took me a few trips to Thailand to know that there was a network of taxi drivers linked to the organized sex-workers' market. They were connected to pimps and individual sex workers. And just about any single man visiting the city was assumed to be seeking an active nightlife and plenty of sex.

Finally, some 45 minutes after leaving the airport, I was at my hotel in the Asoke area of Sukhumvit, a congested part of the metropolis. This area, for some unknown reason, had a visible presence of South Asians, a majority of Indians, some of whom were as noisy as the ones back in Delhi. As I alighted from the taxi and picked up my bags, I could sense them staring at my short postbox-red kurta, black-and-white stripped pyjama pants and the rainbow-coloured leather wrist piece. Damn! I felt I was back home! I guess my travel agent assumed I would be comfortable with 'my own'—Indians—not knowing that for the next eight days, I was seeking liberation from them.

I quickly moved to another hotel in an area where the number of Indians and other South Asians were said to be few. On reaching there, I was welcomed with smiles and greetings from the Thai staff. Some smiles led to eye contact and even my gaydar (the queer ability to spot another gay person) going off, as a bellboy and I glanced at each other briefly. For a moment, I felt he was asking whether I wanted something—whether I wanted him. I wasn't wrong. When he delivered my bags, he smiled and posed a question in broken English: 'You like?' My expression was a puzzled one. So, he pointed to himself and repeated, 'You like, I come to you?'

He was a beautiful man, slim and waif-like, spotless smooth skin and a smile that could light up any blue mood or a happy one too. He lifted his red shirt, part of his uniform, to show me his abs, indicating that I could have them, the whole of him actually. Had this offering come to me a trip or two later, I would have probably pushed him against the wall, helped him remove his shirt and made the most of the privacy the room offered.

At that point, though, conditioned by the 'morals' of Delhi, the class system and its trappings, I smiled and said I was tired and declined the offer. I did regret doing so within minutes and somehow didn't have the courage to call for him later that day. I convinced myself there were more men to see, more days in hand, as my holiday had only just started.

Before reaching Bangkok, I had spent a bit of time on a gay dating app, making a local connection with a young Thai man called Paul. 'Like Paul Smith,' he had said, smiling, referring to the renowned fashion designer. He and I met on my first evening in Bangkok. He was a pleasant person, a scientist by profession and spoke English quite fluently, and that, I realized, wasn't common amongst the local gay community.

While Paul wasn't a date or a person I wished to sleep with, I wasn't sure why he met me. Just about anyone I had interacted with online usually looked for at least a hook-up. Paul didn't seem to be seeking that. Even though I was a complete stranger to him, he was helpful, guiding me to gay places I would soon go to (none with him). What was odd, though, was that on the two occasions we met, he waited outside my hotel, not wanting to come in.

Finally, I asked why he did that. 'The hotel staff may think I am a money-boy,' he explained, 'maybe you think like that too,' he carried on, attempting to say that he sought nothing material or financial from me.

Apparently, gay boys, particularly those who were unemployed or had part-time jobs, made themselves available to tourists or *falang*s (foreigners) for money or even the comfort of a hotel room, free food and entertainment. Paul wished to be seen as an independent person and a professional, while also clarifying that he wasn't against sex workers or money-boys, as it was 'a job, a service to people'. Just that he didn't wish to be typecast as one of them, particularly since he had the monies to pay for sex, like a falang.

'Is that why you haven't been to any of the gay places with me either?' I asked as he drew a map for me of gay hotspots for tourists seeking Thai men, and Thais seeking falangs. Paul said that wasn't the reason. According to him, if any Thai boy saw us—Paul and I—together, they'd think us a pair, a couple out on a date. 'No one will come to you, not even a money-boy,' he said, smiling, seemingly aware that my eyes were roving, on the lookout.

Soon after Paul left for his home in Chiang Mai, the northern part of Thailand, I headed out to the popular gay area just off Silom Road, the heart of the city. I looked around and was stunned by the near-absolute gayness around me. I was told, and it is probably true, that over 50 per cent of the population in this area was queer!

There were two main lanes—Soi 2 and 4—that housed frequently visited gay outlets—restaurants, bars, massage centres, beauty parlours, karaoke bars and discos. Gay tourists often dined at the Telephone Pub & Restaurant on Soi 4, heading to DJ Station on Soi 2 around 11:00 p.m. to catch a drag show and dance. A few years later, there was GOD (Guys On The Dancefloor) that saw the crowd come in once DJ Station closed at 2:00 a.m. The parallel street, Surawongse Road, which had a famous Jim Thomson showroom at its corner, was known for go-go bars, sex shows and boutique gay-run guest houses and hotels.

I was told these weren't the only gay spots in the city. There were lots more, some that were frequented only by Thais who were looking for their own kind. There were beer places, hip-hop bars, cafes, book and sex toy stores, spas, saunas and dark rooms. Then there were countless gay-owned boutiques, parlours, tailoring stores and so on, dotting the city with queer skills for all to consume.

I was overwhelmed by the sheer expanse, access and thriving gay life. Coming from a city and period of deprivation where we celebrated a Tuesday gay night as an achievement and step forward, it was unreal to find places that were LGBTQIA+ focussed, and open every day and night. Yet, I felt watched as I walked down Silom Road and onto Soi 4. I felt conscious of myself, a bit awkward and not comfortable.

When I look back on that day, I am sure no one was staring at me. It was the perils of a Delhi existence, where I feared being found out, as my sexuality was still a secret. So, even though I was on a street that was openly gay and not odd to the city, the area and its surroundings, Delhi still lurked in my mind like a hangover resulting from an overdose of rashly mixed drinks. I was, obviously, conscious of my sexuality.

That evening was spent at the oldest gay bar and restaurant in Asia—the Telephone Pub & Restaurant. Situated towards the middle of the lane, on the left-hand side, it had its uniqueness. Every table and all the seats at the two rectangular bars had a phone attached to them. Each phone had a number and was only for calls within the restaurant. You could pick up the phone, dial someone you fancied and see where it went. I, however, didn't try it this first time.

It was a busy night. I struggled to find a stool at the bar, squeezing myself in. I wasn't the type who'd easily strike a conversation with a stranger, but I did. To be honest, the conversation was initiated by a Thai man, Thong, who spoke a little English, enough to introduce me to a Danish man who was sitting at a dining table, sharing it with some of the cutest boys I had ever seen. His name was Helmer, and he was two years older than me. He was a large person, with a fair complexion, round face and a little bit of golden blonde hair on an otherwise exposed, balding scalp.

Helmer was attracted to Thai men. It was the main reason he had moved to Bangkok from a small village in Denmark. He had taken up a job as a teacher in a school just outside the city, in a place called Bangna. He was pleased by the number of gay places the city had, the endless massage centres and the 24-hour retail chain, 7-Eleven. 'You could get anything you want at any hour,' he told me with great excitement. This was not how life was in Denmark or in most European countries, with the exception of Netherlands, he said.

Yet, there was a lot that left him angry about Thais. To start with, it was their inability to speak English. He also didn't like the loud music at the restaurant, where the decibel was upped just after 10:00 p.m. every night. Then the night markets left too little space for people to walk on a pavement, he complained. The open sale of porn videos and sex toys on the streets was an immoral act 'that would not happen in my country,' he exclaimed, expressing an aversion to sex work too.

'This is their culture, isn't it?' I commented, without getting into any details, as I was merely an uninformed visitor, not a resident. In any case, I had no reason to be peeved as such with Bangkok or Thais.

There was beauty in the chaos and congestion that I encountered in the night markets, the tiny lanes and the busy gay bars I was at. I enjoyed the loud music. I admired the energy of people and the delight of urinating in gay toilets, where seeing and showing an organ was an easy gesture of friendliness, a conversation starter for some. I was fascinated with the way many Thai gay men tried to tempt if not seduce others around them with their eyes, smiles, partly unbuttoned shirts that they wore tight, revealing their nipples, and pants that hugged their body in a manner that did justice to the shape of their booty.

To me, everything I saw and experienced was all very liberating. It was exciting not knowing the boundaries, the extent to which I could go, the discomfort and comfort of growing as a person and as a gay man.

I suppose, this was the perfect mindset for me to carry to the popular beach town of Pattaya, which was a 90-minute drive from Bangkok, a place I was to go to the next day.

THREE

PATTAYA

Situated around 150 kilometres south of the Thai capital, Pattaya was often called 'sin city' and 'sex city', encapsulated best by a line on a T-shirt that read: 'Good guys go to heaven, bad guys go to Pattaya'. A humorous take, it explained what attracted men (mostly heterosexuals) to the beach town and how easy it was to get or buy sex in this part of Thailand.

I was staying at a hotel called the Siam Bayshore View that was located at the end of the beach road, facing the Gulf of Thailand. I had absolutely no idea that the rear exit of the hotel was adjacent to the famous Walking Street where almost all retail outlets were sex shops, with women and lady boys on offer as well as sex toys. There were a handful of beauty stores, Boots stones, ice-cream parlours and sexual health kiosks with condoms, lubricants as well as other products that added to the excitement of sexual activity.

Not too far from there, just off the inner parallel road of the beach road, was Boyz Town: two lanes dominated by gay bars, restaurants, discos, massage centres, hotels, and go-go bars. The streets, interestingly, were connected through a bylane, creating a C-shaped line of queer hang-outs.

As I entered the first of two lanes, the sense of feeling watched, the self-conscious being that I was, returned. I sort of overcame that inhibition by pretending to talk on my mobile phone, avoiding eye contact with anyone, acting oblivious of where I was, like I were a lost straight man, not knowing the area was essentially for gay people. Every time I think of this act, I laugh to myself.

At seven in the evening, as it were, I was one of the few customers, making it difficult for me to go unnoticed by the boys and men working at the various gay places in that lane. They called out, some of them even tried to hold my hand, saying 'come here', 'drink with me', 'we have many boys', smiling and winking, trying to lure me in. I walked directly to a place called Panorama. I had heard about it from Thong, the night before in Bangkok. It was at the corner, where the first street connected with the bylane, sitting at the L. An open restaurant-cum-bar, the seating was strategic and well thought out, as it provided a view of the men walking through both the main street in front and the bylane.

In a very short time, I learnt that just about every person visible who wasn't a customer was up for sale, from the waiters serving drinks and food to the cashier. All one had to do was to pay the bar a tiny sum of ฿200 (around ₹220 then) to take a waiter out. Any other cost was entirely at the discretion of the boy and his customer or client.

I wasn't aware of this immediately though, not until Pop, a mildly muscular, slightly tanned, round-faced 24-year-old, with hair that was to some degree longer than a convict in jail, started a conversation with me. He spoke English, quite a bit of it, in fact. He was curious and asked me a lot about myself—where I was from, what my work was and whether I was on a holiday. He was desperate to go out that evening and hoped I would be his saviour from boredom and the work he was doing at Panorama. However, if I were to pay for anyone to have a little bit of fun with, I would have gone for another guy, someone cute, less assertive, with longer hair, sunken cheeks and more visible shoulder blades (one of my weaknesses), not Pop.

'Please take me out. Everyone will think you have rejected me if you don't. They think I am ugly, my skin colour is dark,' he painfully admitted, letting me know that Thais were racist too, obsessed with the fair skin of South Koreans, a benchmark of beauty. It was for waiters, go-go boys and anyone available to keep potential customers interested in them. If a conversation between a buyer and seller lasted around a minimum of 10 minutes, and the two had a drink together (which Pop and I did), the expectation was that they would leave together.

Being the customer and a foreigner, however, I had the privilege and power to shift my eyes to someone else, invite that person to my table and ignore Pop. It was like window shopping, distracted and undecided due to the abundance of options, and the heartlessness of financial transactions. But somehow, I didn't wish to do that, not wanting to reduce Pop to an inanimate fast-moving consumer goods or a product sitting on a shelf in a store! I knew what rejection felt like, and in any case, I had no plans for that evening.

So, I stepped out with him after paying a bill that had three items listed on it—a Smirnoff vodka, Simba beer and Pop. Surprised to find the young man's name on the tab, I looked at the cashier quizzingly. He just smiled, 'Pop is for you tonight!'

Unfamiliar with this busy little town, I let Pop guide me from one street to another. There was a warmth about him, an easy calm and an energy that transmitted positivity. He knew every nook and corner of Pattaya and, most importantly, liked music. And to my delight, it wasn't the sound of disco we could hear coming out of the dance and go-go place that gave him joy. He liked the blues! 'The blues?' I asked, surprised.

For most part of my queer life, I felt like an outcast at most gay parties, since disco was said to be gay music. If it wasn't disco, it was the new wave sound of Madonna from the 80s that was played, or Club and House, all that saw the rise of technology and digital, partly replacing the charm of analog sounds and the authenticity attached to real instruments. Not that I disliked Madonna, Donna Summers, Village People or disco music as such, it is just that rock, swing, folk and the blues, genres I had taken to, were supposed to be the interest of heterosexuals, representing some sort of masculinity. It made my preferences in artists and songs appear odd and awkward at parties and clubs, like I weren't loyal enough to the community.

Pop broke the mould and other fixed ideas of being gay, of what we wear, listen to and what sports we play. 'Only a few of us think of fashion and make-up. American television and films say we have to be dressed in expensive clothes, wear luxury branded shoes and a lot of make-up. We, in Thailand, like T-shirts and jeans. We like our traditional clothes too,' he said, pointing at a wrap-around cotton pyjama worn by a masseur standing at the corner of the street.

He also played football, as did many other local gay men. This was a game that was never really associated with the gay community. The interest, if any, was usually as a spectator and television audience, ogling at fit men wearing tight shorts that occasionally revealed the shape of their endowment, turning the popular sport into what we flippantly called 'soft porn'. Some of his friends spent time on the basketball court too. And about a year later, I realized that the very rough and masculine combat sport of Thai boxing, called Muay Thai, could be queered, as I saw in the real-life story of Parinya Charoenphol, a trans woman, in the film *Beautiful Boxer*.

'Be yourself, Khun Sharif. No worry, no stress, don't follow media, cinema, make your own choices,' was Pop's offering of wisdom to me that night. He added one more pearl, a simple yet valuable element of life that most counsellors and mental health experts would recommend and reiterate over a decade later, 'Being happy is what matters the most.'

While having this conversation, we reached the middle of a congested section of the sex market, the place where Pop's favourite blues bar was. It had an incredibly talented blues to swing band on stage, covering the likes of BB King, Buddy Guy, Taj Mahal, Aretha Franklin, Bill Haley and John Lee Hooker. There were women serving drinks, hoping to find clients, just like it was at Panorama. Even though we were the outsiders here, the only gay men in the straight bar, the servers welcomed us and in a lighter vein, asked if we'd like something 'extra', meaning sex or a massage or both.

After a few drinks, Pop took out a tiny pill from a plastic Ziploc bag and offered me half of it. I refused to consume what I believe was ecstasy or E, a synthetic drug that is said to act as a central nervous system stimulant. I didn't do drugs. I hadn't even smoked a cigarette in all of my years. I didn't roll joints either at that time. It was only three or four years later that I had a few drags of weed and hash, enjoying the occasional puff, not wishing or wanting to be a habitual consumer of cigarettes or joints.

Although it was a healthy choice and a way to avoid what were considered addictions, my decision had a different basis altogether. I was petrified of drugs, uncomfortable with alcohol, fearing the possibility of losing control of myself and my senses. I suppose, I feared being a person I didn't know, not wishing to let go enough from what was familiar, or that I had come to expect myself to behave in a certain way that was considered well-mannered and civil.

So, even when Pop placed the drug in front of me again, offering it in a coy and pleading manner, insisting it was safe, that I need not be scared and it would add to our excitement,

I declined to take it, leaving him the full pill to consume.

Notwithstanding this decision that appeared to disappoint Pop, it was a refreshing night of sex, making out in a bathtub, enjoying warm water from the rain shower and the cuddles that followed in bed. I don't know whether it was his mastery over the art of serving customers that made the night memorable. Or if it was the drug at work and the alcohol that we drank, which meant he would have been sexually wonderful with anyone, not just me. The way my mind buzzed with questions, it was quite clear that I was hoping for validation—for him to say I was worth it, that we had a chemistry, that I was good in bed and would be so even without the booze and drugs that could have made me a blur in his mind and memory.

Pop left the next morning. He didn't seek a penny and was grateful that I had taken him out of Panorama. 'You are nice, not like other falangs,' he said, turning back to look at me while exiting the room, smiling and eliciting a smile from me too. We reached out to each other, hugged and kissed. 'We meet again before you go?' he asked, whispering gently in my ear. I whispered back, 'yes,' holding back the excitement of being appreciated, accepted, desired and wanted.

We met the same evening but not at Panorama, although we had to go there later to pay another ฿200 as per the rules, accounting for his absence from the bar. We had dinner in the large courtyard of the hotel, with the Gulf of Thailand before us. We watched the sunset and listened to the waves lightly caress the cemented shoreline. It was what was typically called a romantic setting, the kind that two lovers would revel in, a place where Pop and I seemed to develop a familiarity and fondness for each other.

He knew what gay relationships were like as well as one-night stands, sex work and being an escort. On two occasions as an escort—that involves eating, drinking and sleeping with a tourist besides being a guide—Pop had found himself in love and then in a relationship. 'I even lived in Frankfurt in Germany with my boyfriend who was earlier my client,' he shared with a bit of gusto. That is how he had become more conversant with English and aware of a world beyond his country.

The relationship, however, died out as the German found other Thai boys to entertain him during their return visits to Thailand. 'He could find anyone and could leave me whenever he wished. If this happens to me when I am older, I will not be able to serve as a money-boy or escort,' he revealed with utter frankness, admitting that youthfulness had its virtue in a market that catered to the middle-aged to aging tourists who fancied younger men. I, as it were, was one of them!

His experience with a Frenchman had been the same. That boyfriend, he said, was always tempted by beautiful men, breaking promises he made to Pop, sleeping with multiple people, often without any care for sexual health and safety. The Frenchman would buy gifts and 'throw money at me' in exchange, 'as though I was worth nothing', and that hurt him a lot. 'I could earn money, too, even in Grasse, where we lived, but being a foreigner, I was always an outsider to the escort service network,' he revealed. With no feet to stand on as such, the only option for a dignified life, he explained, was to return to Pattaya, putting an end to that relationship.

I was to hear more such stories of indignity and economic inequality from other Thai men and back home in India too. What shocked me, though, were other forms of power play, that Pop had had clients who were physically violent, assaulting him in the name of kinkiness. He could not fight back or stop the person from attacking him. Being a poor local Thai in an economy catering to tourism, he'd most likely be judged as the guilty one, carrying the burden of class heirarchies and the buyer–seller equation that was defined by terms such as 'customer is king' and 'money talks'. According to him, 'The falang can call the police and the hotel staff, and lodge a complaint of robbery or anything,' revealing the vulnerabilities attached to his work.

In Pop's stories, I found similarities with a large number of Indian families that were guilty of domestic violence. I saw Pop as a woman, a wife pigeonholed into the role of a homemaker, serving and reporting to a patriarch, the husband, who could do whatever he wanted to her, irrespective of her wishes, desires or consent. After all, he was the breadwinner and provider, and she, at his beck and call.

If Pop's work was part of the unorganized sector, with no specified means to put an economic value to his service, women are unaware that their unpaid work, mostly domestic, is equivalent to around 40 per cent of the GDP.[2] So, just like Pop, the silence of women in instances of violence and abuse has a

---

[2]Samuel, Vineet John, 'Unpaid Work: Women and the Burden of Unpaid Labour', Down To Earth, 31 January 2019, https://tinyurl.com/mpn9fcvd. Accessed on 11 October 2019.

lot to do with how society views their voice and dignity, if any. It has to do with socioe-conomics too. When Pop exclaimed, 'Who'd listen to me?' I could hear the exact same lines being said by women who knew they'd be fighting a losing battle, even if it were a good fight.

Pop and I sauntered down Walking Street, holding each other's hands, tightening our grip as we stepped closer to my hotel. 'Not everyone has to fall in love, and not all stories end like mine, Sharif,' he said, sensing that I seemed quite troubled by his experiences. 'There are kind men who have fallen in love with a woman or man they met at a go-go bar,' he said. Some of them were well-settled, 'returning to Thailand with their husbands, wives and children, spending weeks and months with their Thai in-laws, becoming part of a large family,' he told me.

That night with Pop was sexually less active, less lustful, perhaps due to a certain comfort that we now seemed to share. He left the next morning as I prepared for a day trip to see the corals an hour away into the gulf. 'If you want to meet me, please call or see me at Panorama,' he whispered, expectedly, hugging me tight. We held each other with a definitive sense of care. As we let go, and I saw him walking away towards the elevators, I got this strange feeling that this was perhaps the last time we were meeting.

The boat ride to view the corals was largely a pointless one, given that there was hardly anything visible, just a minute of a glimpse of corals far off, somewhere close to a desolate island. What was interesting, though, was the mix of people on this journey—Europeans, Russians and Americans, and quite a few

Indian couples, newly married, evident from the red bangles and mehndi on their hands and arms.

Over the years, I have noticed how many Indian couples seek some kind of liberation and modernity during their honeymoons and holidays in Thailand. While the mangalsutra and sindoor usually remains intact, their saris and salwar kameezes are tucked away in their suitcases until their flights home or their return to the daily grind of being wives, daughters-in-law and homemakers.

I recognized some of the Indian faces on the trip that day, having seen them earlier, shopping for tight T-shirts, ripped jeans, sunglasses, fashion accessories and shoes. It didn't matter if these were knock-offs or fakes. It was good enough to send out the message that they were 'with it', modern and fashionable. For many such couples, this was their first foreign trip—carrying a passport that lost its virginity with a rubber stamp that marked their exit out of India.

As much as they appeared to enjoy the shopping and touring, they were critical of Pattaya and its visible sex market. They commented on the pink-lit open bars where women stood on top of tables, pole dancing. They saw dirt and filth in the women standing at street corners, waiting for a customer. They didn't spare the customers who sought the services of sex workers either, unaware of the needs of old and young men, some who sought a warm hug, who found sex and lust reassuring and therapeutic, probably finding a way out of rejection and loneliness. And I could vouch for that.

These couples, three of them, got together, finding a

connection, talking about 'paap' or 'sin' and the 'sick' world of sex and sex work. They went to the extent of claiming that India had none of this, utterly ignorant or in denial of the many red-light areas in most cities and towns across the country. In 'our culture', they stated, relationships were sacred and sex was only within marriages, such as theirs.

Suddenly, I felt their eyes on me. They stared at my maroon shorts, sleeveless peach T-shirt and multicoloured bead neckpiece and then looked at each other. '*Ye waise hi lagta hain, koi angrez.* Walking Street *main time bitata hoga* (He looks like a foreigner who spends time in Walking Street),' one of them said. It seems they had decided, based on my clothes, that I wasn't Indian but a 'dirty' Englishman or American customer looking for sex on Walking Street. And, of course, they presumed I was heterosexual!

'*Sex-wex aur ye sab to important he nahi hain. Shaadi to do family aur do aatma ka milan hain* (Sex and all isn't important at all. Marriage is the bringing together of two families and souls),' I recall one of the women saying as the rest nodded in agreement in a self-righteous manner. Obviously, they rejected *shareerik sambandh* or physical relationships. I can't but forget how two of the women watched me from the corner of their eyes, probably itching to tell me how soulless I was.

I could be wrong, but these women appeared to be products of arranged marriages, where sex is a duty, a service to the husband and a means to procreate. Even if they weren't, we did belong to a culture that didn't wish to see or appreciate sex as pleasure, or as Seema Anand, the London-based mythologist, an authority on the *Kama Sutra*, says, 'a beauty and art'. In a conversation some two years ago, she explained, 'pleasure was a shakti and lovemaking was an art form.' So, 'you did not just move about mindlessly in bed', as the engagement itself was an understanding of each other's bodies, what excited each other and how to take positions that enhanced the experience of lovemaking or sex.

These couples, I thought, represented a large section of Indians who found discussing sex impolite, degrading and immoral, as it was culturally a taboo, even though they'd spend countless number of hours on a preoccupation called procreation and the 'family way'. I remember smiling to myself as I thought about the Hindi films I had grown up watching, where a kiss was camouflaged by bushes and flowers or the reflection of trees on a windscreen if the couple were in a car. Several generations were left to imagine how we came into this world, like it were some magic and a 'poof, here we are' story.

As a result, it was but natural for any one of us to get embarrassed (our teachers too) during a biology class when information on the vagina, penis and sexual intercourse were hurriedly and sketchily shared. Similarly, buying condoms has always been awkward. Even I had struggled to look into the eyes of a salesman at a medical store, wanting to purchase a pack, as though I was doing something wrong, and it wasn't uncommon for him to smirk or look suspiciously at me. That safe sex was an imperative would never strike the mind of the shopkeeper, just like many riders on two-wheelers who don't think it necessary to wear a helmet. No wonder then, when

India's population touched over 1.1 billion in the year 2006, (38 years after India's first condom, Nirodh, was launched), it was found necessary to have a 'Condom Bindaas Bol' (ask freely) campaign, with a message to not feel shy, hesitant or uncomfortable asking for the protective shield!

In Thailand, however, condoms were placed in the minibars of hotel rooms as part of the menu. Some hotels offered lubricants, sitting prominently with water, tea and coffee, perhaps recognizing everyone's thirst as unique. And if you didn't like the options in your room, there was always a 7-Eleven, Family Mart, Watson and Boots store to literally pick and choose the flavour you preferred. But for these young Indian couples, all of this was evidently too much. I, however, was fascinated and elated.

In fact, I was getting more and more acclimatized with the ubiquitous presence of sex, that it was a service, where attraction to one another was considered human, and to say and show it was 'normal'. Which is why I was agitated that our boat returned past the scheduled time to the crescent-shaped Pattaya beach, that I'd now be late in reaching Panorama.

I rushed to my hotel room much after 7:00 p.m., closer to 8:00. After a quick warm shower, I headed to Panorama, striding in, familiar with the place and space, wanting to make the most of my last night in the beach town. I sat at one of the tables in the first row, looking out for Pop. He wasn't there. 'He go with falang,' I was told by one of the waiters. 'When?' I asked. 'I think he waited for you from 7 o'clock, maybe for an hour,' he replied, 'customer keep asking, he could not say no!'

As much as I felt alone, hurt and jealous, missing my new friend, there was a sense of happiness that sunk in a bit later. It came entirely from the waiter's revelation that Pop had waited for me, delaying his customer, an inappropriate behaviour and a risk in his line of work. As I understood it, Pop had drawn a line between his profession and our friendship, a growing fondness for each other, and would have chosen me over extra money that a client may have offered him!

I could never comprehend how difficult it may have been for him to offer his body, perform with passion and do all that it took to bring a smile on the face of a client. I didn't know how he could and did reserve a friendlier, affectionate self for me after work.

We never met again, as I left for Bangkok early the next morning. We exchanged messages, spoke a few times, unsure of how and when we'd see each other. As it was, distant geographies, our separate lives and the passage of time naturally put a lid on what may have been!

FOUR

A NEW WORLDVIEW

As I entered the Telephone Pub in the evening soon after I returned from Pattaya, I was accosted by an elderly, blue-eyed, large-framed, friendly and jovial man. 'You are new here, meeting Helmer, are you?' A question that surprised me. 'Come with me,' he said, taking me to the first floor, where my Danish friend was sitting, sipping a Coca-Cola, looking down at the ground floor, searching and hopeful he'd find a handsome gay man.

The friendly person was Wayne Waterson, co-owner of the Telephone Pub, often seen sitting on a bar stool next to the entry, meeting and greeting old and new customers. An Australian from Sydney, he had worked in different parts of Southeast Asia, including Singapore, Japan and Bangkok, before deciding to make the Thai capital his home.

His attraction for Asia had begun in the 1960s while working with Qantas Airways, when he had been sent to Singapore to attend the funeral of one of his Singaporean apprentices who had been killed in a motorbike accident. He had then chosen to quit his job with the airline and had got employed with the local government, spending 30 years working with different aviation companies, one of which had allowed him to travel all over the Far East, giving him a greater understanding of different Asian cultures.

He loved food, people and gay life, which is why in the mid-1980s, while working in Japan, he had opened the GB pub in Tokyo that had seen much success and failure as well. In the year 2000, he had moved to Bangkok, and within a couple of years he had invested in the 1987-born Telephone Pub, becoming a co-owner, in which role he had continued till a few years ago, when he retired. He had a spirited equation with the team. He humoured them, and on special occasions and at his whim, he'd take them out for a round of drinks at DJ Station once the restaurant closed for the night. His generosity and bonhomie extended to weekend trips and night-outs in Pattaya as well. It was a culture of solidarity, classlessness, connected by sexuality and the 'need' for happiness.

Wayne was kind to me too, sharing gay guides, discount coupons and even handing me a lifetime loyalty card for the pub. This translated into a 10 per cent discount at the outlet and the many affiliated gay places in Bangkok, Pattaya and Phuket. 'Enjoy this,' he told me, knowing full well that I would get hooked to Thailand and its openness to our community.

Having lived in Singapore for three decades, he was familiar with several Indian and Malay families and gay men who lived there. He was conscious of the extreme conservativeness and homophobia within the Indian and Malay community as well as the scarce liberalism that allowed nourishment for love within a family. I guess, aware that I came from Delhi and was living a life with Section 377 still in place, he was extra affectionate and protective towards me, initiating a friendship that we still have and cherish.

Wayne was a veteran on love, how relationships evolve and what it is to be with an Asian—Singaporean or Thai. He had a long relationship with Ismail, an Indian–Malay Muslim who he had met in Singapore in 1972. There had been a gap in their relationship for some years when Wayne had moved to Bangkok, their friendship, however, remains intact to this day. While running the Telephone Bar, he had been drawn towards a young local nicknamed Ice. Deeply in love, the two had been least troubled by each other's popularity amongst Thais and foreigners alike, leading to the occasional sexcapade. 'Love goes beyond the body, beyond the physical,' was his reading of true love.

Ice has been with Wayne for over 20 years and is still very much part of his life. Ismail has had a devoted relationship with Wayne for almost 50 years now. In 2015, Ismail became his primary caregiver when he was diagnosed with neck cancer, spending hours in the hospital in Sydney and at home, cooking Singaporean and Malay delicacies. 'He has been by my side 100 per cent of the time through seven months of radiation and chemotherapy,' he told me, adding that their relationship remains rock solid.

While both Ice and Wayne have had their occasional flings, their love for each other has an immeasurable depth, intangible yet unbreakable. About a year ago, during the Covid-19 pandemic, one of Ice's aged men fell sick. Wayne got into action, trying to save that man's life, footing huge hospital bills without any hesitation. 'Guess what, Sharif, our love has grown even more ever since,' he told me.

I have learnt a lot from him, not just about relationships but about the 'Thai way'. He said that to love a Thai person meant you'd have to love Thailand and its culture. 'This is the guiding principle and no ordinary learning,' Wayne remarked on one of the evenings I was at the pub. Agreeing with him were several other foreigners and a Thai scholar, who had all pulled up chairs, joining the conversation. The foreigners, now expats, had chosen to live in Bangkok and neighbouring Bangna, leaving their homes in Europe, US, Australia and New Zealand. The Thai scholar, named Boe, had settled down with one of them.

During this first visit to Bangkok and over a period of time I have observed that the Thai way is unique in so many ways. For example, every building has a beautiful space for Buddha, a protective spirit house, often elevated, sitting in a corner and always visible—at banks, malls, restaurants, residential complexes, offices, massage parlours, sex show outlets and go-go bars. 'If Buddha is everywhere, there is no sin as such,' I was told, 'everything is blessed.' To pay obeisance to Buddha, to feed monks and to donate to temples is considered good karma, a negation of bad or wrong acts.

Although Westernized clothing such as sleeveless T-shirts and tops, short skirts and hot pants are commonly worn by women and men, entering a Buddhist temple in such an attire is unacceptable. You're asked to cover your exposed shoulders and given a wrap-around piece of cloth to conceal your legs.

While the birth of a child is a celebration, as in most parts of the world, so is the demise of someone. People cry and grieve, but the seeing off of the soul, is somewhat festive and in variance with how one mourns in most other countries, including mine. It isn't peculiar or odd to find the bereaved family smiling, being hospitable, after all, the soul has been liberated.

Thais focus on happiness and that lies even in the smallest things such as Som Tam (the much-loved raw papaya salad), a mindless conversation, an animation film, lipstick and anything that appear mundane and trivial to us busy outsiders. It also lies in the ability to serve and make others happy, which is why working at a massage parlour and being a sex worker isn't disrespected, as the ultimate goal of providing happiness is being met! Massage, as a practice of healing and serving, is so engrained in Thais that just about everyone knows the basics, learning from *wats* (temples) across the country or from parents, if they belonged to families that believed in handing down the skill and practice.

Most of the working class in Bangkok, particularly those in the service industry, hail from families involved in farming, owning large pieces of land (for some, their only personal wealth). To them, nothing matters more than home. If their family calls them back, they'd quit their job immediately, giving no notice, not once bothered about a financial loss or the loss of their reputation as a worker.

Another Thai cultural nuance is gratefulness. Whatever they get is Buddha-given or from their King, who they worshipped at that time with nearly equal devotion. That is why most Thais don't nag customers for tips. This sense of gratitude extends to several celebrations including a birthday where what matters most is to thank Buddha by visiting a temple and taking a monk's blessings, not a gift or the symbolic cutting of a cake.

At the core of existence, coexistence, human interaction and life in general is the belief that: things are the way they are; they are meant to be that way. The often-used phrase is *mai pen rai*. In colloquial Thai, it translates to 'it doesn't matter' and 'it is okay', or even a more elaborate, 'no problem, it doesn't matter'. If I were to take this phrase and place it into a Vedic context, it would mean everything is destined or predestined, irrespective of our actions or karma in our current life. Boe, who had studied the Vedas as well as the evolution of Buddhism, found that Thai philosophy overlaps or is derived from the Vedas and elements of Hinduism. The idea of karma, though, is a bit more emphasized in their local practice of Buddhism: keep doing good and accept the fruit of God, even if it isn't what we expect or desire.

The next day, I visited the Sri Mahamariamman Temple on Silom Road, a Tamil temple built in 1879. Apparently, the place of worship was a creation of gemstone traders who had managed to shift base from the Tamil region in South

India to the safer, uncolonized Thailand. While the temple was a replica of Tamil architecture as seen in the triangular-shaped tops, archaic large solid wood doors and multicoloured brightness, I spotted Buddha placed comfortably amongst a number of Hindu gods. Buddhism, I saw and absorbed, has never been averse to Hinduism, as Hindu deities have been seen as protectors of Buddha, which is why it is normal to have Brahma, Vishnu, Ganesh and Indra at a Thai Buddhist temple. It is also the reason why Boe said he found 'the Indian reaction to homosexuality quite out of sync with its religion,' hoping I had something to explain.

As argued by some historians, scholars, liberals and sections of the queer community, colonization has done a lot of damage to queer rights and social status with the imposition of Section 377. The prudishness of the British monarch that was adopted by the dominant Indian middle class led to a colonized version of who we were and are as people and a culture. As Dr Alka Pande said at the Rainbow Lit Fest, the earlier 'rulers' and 'invaders', the Mughals, part of what she called Islamic India, from the eighth century, 'were pleasure-seekers, they were hedons', unlike the Englishmen.[3]

I have often wondered what life would have been without the British Raj. Would we have any dignity and place in society or just continue to be a part of a mythical narrative, a piece of art in a temple, a story here or there?

---

[3]'Even the Muslim Era in India Was One with Pleasures of Sex and Desire: Dr Alka Pande', YouTube, https://youtu.be/-sFPlAPTGyQ. Accessed on 20 September 2022.

My friend, Nandini Sengupta, who is an author and senior journalist, said that to understand India is to see its history and traditions as a tapestry of a million colourful skeins, each warp and weft a unique point of view, all coming together to weave the big picture. 'For every story that our past offers us, there is a counter-narrative too—for every Akbar, there's a Chand Bibi or Durgawati, for every Aurangzeb, a Lachit Borphukan, for every Ashoka, a Kharavela,' she said.

Our colonial skew, she argued, 'Tells us that patriarchy ensured women in India had a marginal role in antiquity. And yet, there are so many smart, powerful, learned and popular queens who pop up in our history—from Prabhavati Gupta to Rudramadevi, from Didda to Durgawati, from Tarabai to Abakka Chowta.' Their narrative, though, she underlined, 'still begs retelling because the dominant story still is the one told by a man.'

Boe agreed and observed that history has to be re-accessed, rewritten and reviewed; it isn't just about whether a man or woman was the author of a certain history, it is to do with the ethnicity of the historian as well as the role of the subject. In addition, just like the press did in some countries, historians should declare their ideological and political party affiliations, as well as their source of funding of research, if any, so that readers are aware of possible prejudice. 'Maybe the writers you've studied should have said they had a Victorian bent of mind!' Boe remarked in a jocular manner. On a more serious note, he pointed out that perhaps we had fewer historians earlier, and, now, with more research and finance, we could see multiple views on events and lives of the past being included. 'This can prove to be contentious, beneficial or problematic,' he added.

It was in 1956 that Thailand did away with its sodomy law, decriminalizing homosexuality, giving the community a long history of legitimacy. As a nation that was never colonized, it managed to retain a certain kind of androgynous form of attire and hairstyle till the mid-nineteenth century. But that was to change. 'As we developed and got more exposed to the West, we adopted some of their conservatism in behaviour, morality and laws,' said Boe, implying that there are pushbacks to a greater integration of the community into the larger system of governance, industry, healthcare and media.

Like any other nation, the 'land of smiles' isn't perfect. There is sadness, deprivation, corporate and political crimes, accidents on the roads, sexual assaults, as well as a well-hidden and allegedly powerful drug mafia. 'The mafia is concealed and underground, an immoral and criminal act that is part of the underbelly, similar to many other cities,' a local journalist friend of mine said.

Irrespective of all its flaws, I flew out of Bangkok with a sense of joy of having found a safe space just four hours away. The joy was such that there was the angst of returning to my resident city and the pain of separation of leaving Thailand. There were tears rolling down my cheeks, and the distress was such that it was hard to see anything good in Delhi.

The chaos at the Delhi airport that I had been used to seemed terribly ugly now. I was agitated by the shouting parents and children, the pushing and shoving, blaring car horns and the traffic police using high decibel megaphones to clear the bottleneck outside the airport. Every tiny thing seemed like an irritant, be it the doorbell in the morning, a book moved out of place on a shelf, a corner in my room that wasn't properly cleaned, wiper marks on the car windshield, the quality of the vegetables. Nothing seemed okay.

It took me five or six days to calm down, to return to being a more tolerant and accepting person, the kind I was prior to my visit to Thailand. But a week or 10 days later, I felt miserable once again, although for a different reason, a grave one—the murder of a gay man, Pushkin Chandra. The press, in what was typical of itself then, hounded the gay community, turning the crime into a 'queer sort of murder', a 'queer' killing, and nothing that was straight and honest. There was a focus on a cache of photographs found in Pushkin's home rather than who killed him and why. There were class angles in focus too, with leading publications using terms such as 'gigolo trail' and 'Sordid Sleazeberg', demonizing our community, failing to find out how we had to live, the social mobility amongst us and the compulsions of secrecy.

The kind of reporting we saw was similar to how the media had written about a raid conducted on the community in Lucknow three years earlier. It was evil, salacious, profiling the community as sex perverts, going to the extent of questioning our mental state. Our place in their worldview was such that the 2001 petition seeking the reading down of Section 377 by Naz Foundation was rejected by some prominent newspapers by not reporting it, and a handful of others just limiting the development to a few tiny paragraphs and diary items.

Pushkin's murder had occurred after a late-night party in Sadiq Nagar, organized as a farewell to a gay man from Europe. There had been a large number of queer people, including diplomats, in attendance. The information we had was that Pushkin, who had also been there, had left with another man, and a third person had joined them later. What had happened after that was not known, even the media did not have any detailed report on the sequence of events. The police, however, had left most of us jittery, including those that had not attended the get-together or had known Pushkin, making random calls to friends, family and those who had attended the party. The law enforcers took possession of several mobile phones to access their directories.

As a community, we pulled back on parties, cruising, casual meetings at coffee shops, and more or less rushed back into the closet, for the fear of the press, the police and society. Even legitimate programmes on safe sex and AIDS focussed on men having sex with men, were curtailed.

Anxious and cautious, most of us didn't call each other over our mobile phones for weeks, not sure if it was safe to do so, wondering if our phones had been tapped. Even my mother was worried by the profiling of gay men in the press, knowing full well how the word 'sex' played out in society. She knew several of my friends who had been summoned by the Defence Colony Police Station, a few kilometres away from our residence. 'Will they call you?' she asked, worried as any loving mother would be. 'No', I said. 'Are they safe, your friends?'

she wished to know, keen that the small gay group I was part of didn't break up or collapse into oblivion.

It was around then that Helmer phoned me, checking in on me, whether I was mentally and emotionally stable. 'So far, so good,' I replied. It was a relief talking to him and to some of my newfound friends in Thailand, all concerned about what they had been reading in the newspapers. When I told them Pushkin's home was 500 meters away from mine, they suggested I pack up and leave, which was nothing but an overreaction, I thought then.

But it was Helmer who felt that I must have a short- or medium-term plan to move to Bangkok, explore opportunities in that city and find a nice Thai guy to live with, 'Wouldn't you want to consider that?' he asked. I did. I was fascinated by the thought itself. What would it feel like if this was real—finding a job in Thailand, the prospect of liberation, finding love and settling down, I wondered.

FIVE
PRIDE

Thailand, from what I had seen, appeared to be a country where it would be easy for foreigners to find a job, given the welcoming nature of its people towards tourists. The large number of expatriates happily settled in that country, holding important positions in multinational and local companies, was another reason for me to believe I stood a chance. Sitting with friends over drinks, we assumed that my English speaking and writing skills were significant advantages, like they were in our country. After all, international brands and tourists would prefer to engage in what is the most widely spoken language in the world.

To my dismay, however, Thailand was much like China, where English was primarily a language of convenience. It carried no privilege, class or advantage, and was merely important if it were central to a job and business. While local Thais learnt the language for their specific role and career, it took me several visits to notice and realize how broken English was good enough, and how the lack of proficiency in the language did not impact tourism or business in general.

The small kingdom, I learnt, was quite a wealthy one and had a strong economy that had been growing mightier with time. It was built on and around tourism, which contributed about 15 per cent of GDP,[4] followed by agriculture, with almost half of its population employed in the fields and related businesses. It also had a good-sized manufacturing industry, electronics being a key part of it.

Given that my work experience at that point in time was in the fields of publishing, journalism and research, my chances were definitely limited. The Thai market didn't need journalists or content writers, and not foreigners, for sure. The possibilities for a foreigner lay in the fields of trade and other kinds of businesses, none of which were endearing for me, leave alone the fact that I would be a green horn, dismissed before reaching the threshold.

To be a teacher, too, an option I was considering on Helmer's recommendation, required additional certifications to qualify. 'The only way to move here for a foreigner is a job transfer to this region as an international posting. The other means is to have money, invest in a local business or set up something that has a market for Thais or South Asians,' an Indian journalist

[4]Theparat, Chatrudee, 'Tourism to continue growth spurt in 2017', *Bangkok Post*, 17 February 2017.

based in Bangkok said, placing the lay of the land before me, giving me an idea of where I stood—seemingly, nowhere!

'Will things open up with the India–Thailand Free Trade Agreement (FTA)?' asked Helmer, referring to a series of talks that had started between the two countries earlier that year. I had my doubts, since the FTA was all about trade, not services and manpower. Nations, in any case, were becoming increasingly wary of opening their borders to foreign nationals. Hence, on every occasion I spoke to Helmer on this subject, I felt downcast, as nothing had worked out till then for me, not even a part-time job or a work profile that gave me the best of both worlds—Thailand and my home in Delhi with my mother.

Helmer taught at one of the top schools in that area and could afford a three-bedroom duplex home in a gated housing complex. 'Whatever I want is here,' he said, referring to a supermarket, Burger King and massage parlours, all situated close to his residence. A short drive to the BTS Station ensured he reached the heart of Bangkok—Silom Road—quite easily. Believe me, this was a life that attracted me a lot more than the one I had—a far smaller residence, even a one-room place, and any job that could give me the kind of freedom he had, would do. I was even least bothered about status or stature, in the way we typically attached dignity, or didn't, to a job.

Around 2005, in the month of October, I was surprised by an offer to run Integral PR, a communications and public affairs consultancy headquartered in Delhi, as its CEO. Friends and family saw the post as the fruit of hard work, unaware that I hadn't worked for or aimed to be a CEO of any kind of business. I had zilch experience of running a firm, let alone a public relations (PR) consultancy, an industry that had a love–hate relationship with journalists. If there was anything to write home about, it was that I was perhaps (as people in the industry said) amongst the youngest leaders in the PR and consultancy field, at the age of 36, a rarity until the start-up industry changed the notion of age, leadership and business enterprise.

While learning something new was exciting and I was lucky to have a chairman who looked after the financial affairs of the firm and the paperwork that came with it (an extremely weak spot in my case), I was to acclimatize myself with our regions that were called 'markets'. I was also expected to build a network nationally and internationally, including in Thailand, since India was a market of opportunity! So, while the FTA had little in it for me personally, it was now a business reason to forge ties with the Thai kingdom.

Within days of moving into the new office and a cabin, I had to leave for a conference in Hong Kong. It was early November, and Helmer told me that it was time for Pride. I had never attended a Pride March or any such festival that centred around our LGBTQIA+ identity. So, I flew to Hong Kong via Bangkok and flew out of Hong Kong to Delhi via Bangkok, giving me a total of three nights in the Thai capital. I had high expectations of Pride, given what I had seen online of such gatherings and marches in New York City, San Francisco, London and Sydney. The many floats, the flamboyance, colour, music, dance and an elaborate show of our diversity looked fascinating and yet distant to me until that day, where the real experience was an intangible quantum of emotions.

I had never imagined standing in the middle of a supercity, just four hours away from home, in full public view, unabashedly a gay man, walking down a main street, not feeling watched or judged by people, or for that matter, hated. There were so many of us—several thousand queer people—walking the march, where I felt both lost in the numbers and found in my sense of being. While we danced, gazed at each other, smiled and even cruised for a hook-up or date, local heterosexuals didn't hesitate to join in, laugh along and hug some of us. What gave me a high was the feeling that we owned that space, the street, no longer aliens in the middle of the public. I experienced a sense of belonging—this is where I should be, these are my people! I think I was like a little child in a toy store looking at everything curiously: the distinctive outfits with huge radiant feathers, Pride flags of different sizes and balloons stitched together in a sequence that made them look like the rainbow.

On that day, everything that normally divided and distinguished us as a human race—religion, nationality, language, the size and shape of our bodies, attire, accessories, the colour of our skin—didn't seem to matter. What I felt was the palpable spirit of camaraderie, a strong bond and thread of solidarity and humanity. I guess the popular Thai phrase 'same, same, but different' summed things up!

For around an hour, perhaps longer, I saw the amplification of Pride as it was in the West. Some of the floats had go-go boys waving randomly to us and the audience on the crowded pavements. Drag queens on another one were swaying to the rhythm of music, lip-syncing with perfection. What stood out, though, was the local culture, with gay men, lady boys and lesbians sticking to traditional outfits, including Thai-style gold-sequin headdresses, gowns and fancy wrap-arounds in cotton and silk.

What surprised me, in a pleasant way, was the presence of global and local brands, and even the ownership of some of the floats by companies. I was told that a few of the visible businesses where gay-owned. This got me to believe that gay life was well integrated into the Thai corporate world, whereas the actuality was contradictory, as there was a lot of work left in terms of policymaking within corporations and outside. Bangkok Pride had become 'a show to promote brands', pointed out Boe, explaining why he wasn't present at the annual event, spending time, instead, at smaller, intimate community functions tucked away at a distance from the Pride March. It struck me then that brands and corporations were merely making a quick buck out of the movement, using it as a platform to earn goodwill with a queer consumerbase and talent pool.

While the first Pride in the city had been initiated by gay business leaders, reportedly, since there had been no LGBTQIA+ groups taking the initiative, it had evolved into a festival and party, obscuring the voices of activists seeking equality or claiming rights for the community. The irony was that even I didn't notice the limited presence of slogans clamouring for equal rights, obviously charmed by the fun, frolic and the brief unfettered existence I was experiencing. In a year or so,

Bangkok Pride came to a halt for these very reasons, returning only 11 years later, in 2017, correcting its past follies, having several LGBTQIA+ community groups in the lead, ensuring that corporate money and flamboyance of the event did not overtake the history of the movement, not stealing the purpose of Pride or its specific queer representation of frolic.

What was common across the world was the love–hate relationship and conflict between capitalism/profit and human rights. Activists would often blame corporations for their silence on critical issues of humanity, equality and equity, building equations and relationships with government and political parties that denied us our rights. Advertisements from brands and products usually excluded queer existence, not seeing the community as a stakeholder, were inherently homophobic or didn't wish to upset the majority of their consumers by recognizing us. Of course, this was to change in the years to come, albeit little and very slowly!

Even in India, the debate over freedom and ownership, and the involvement of industry, has been an ongoing one. 'Corporations can't live off our plight, our challenges, bravery and battle,' a committee member of the Delhi Queer Pride (DQP) once told me, exasperated by a few gay men who felt more funds would up the decibel levels and festivities around Pride. So far, barring Mumbai Pride, most other Prides, including Delhi, have fended off overtures from large companies—Indian and foreign—maintaining the political and independent nature of the movement. After all, as many would say, money can corrupt the purity of a movement. It can compromise on the history and plight of many living across the world. It is like arriving at a birthday party, a milestone that is more about a date and not the lived experience to get there. It is a bit like appropriation, taking ownership of something that isn't theirs, added the DQP committee member.

Yet, that didn't mean we'd deprive ourselves of reasons to celebrate our triumphs and braveness. As Debolina Dey, a friend and an English professor at the University of Delhi, once said, 'We can protest, spend hours on streets, but we can party too!'

Around 7:00 p.m. that evening, I headed to what was to become my favourite haunt—yes, the Telephone Pub. The lane was teeming with people, much like the peak-hour local train in Mumbai, no space, bodies rubbing against each other, a pleasurable sensation at times. As I opened the glass door of the bar, I saw several men topless, wearing only swimming trunks or short, tight pants. They were standing in a long row, from the ground floor, going up the stairs, leading to the first floor. They had numbers hanging from their waist. It was an absolute pleasure to the eyes, a feast to watch the firm, chiselled bodies of young Thai men, many of whom were wearing very tight trunks, revealing the shape of things that were otherwise private.

They were all part of a competition that called for no skills as such, as their victory depended on their popularity amongst us customers at the pub. We had to vote by buying red roses and handing them over to the person we preferred. The man with the maximum roses would be declared the winner.

I participated, as it gave me a moment to come up close to the boy who had won the swimming trunk competition earlier in the day, named Chon. I gave him a dozen roses, looked into his eyes and smiled. I could muster the courage to say that I liked him, and he responded, 'Where are you from?' When I told him that I was Indian, he didn't believe it, as he expected someone with darker skin, oblivious of the heterogeneity unique to our nation.

Chon won the popularity competition and after being congratulated and felt up by many foreigners, I was delighted to see him walk through the pub, to the table Helmer, Thong and I were seated at. He didn't think twice before pulling up a chair, picking up my glass of wine, sipping it as though it was his or that I had offered it to him. He obviously knew I liked him and smiled at me when he was heading to our table.

There was a twinkle in his eyes and naughtiness too. Thong, who was sitting on my left, got up and told him to sit next to me. He did so, unhesitatingly, putting his hand on my thigh, gradually bringing it closer to my inner thigh. Very soon, he checked if I had been aroused, which I was, responding to his gentle hand movement, imagining being in bed with him. He put his hand on mine and guided it to his boner, wanting me to hold it tight. I looked at him with half a smile, and whispered in his ear, 'I am top, are you bottom?' The smile and delight on his face disappeared in seconds, aware now that we could at best make out, as I was not ready to bottom for him nor was he ready to give up on his preferred position in bed.

He had the most precious and beautiful body I had ever seen, with four abs, not an ounce of fat, a warm smile, a strong and shapely femur, nothing I had come close to touching ever in my life. I was hoping he would say yes to making out, sleeping together or having some oral sex!

Instead, he gave me a hug and a kiss on my lips before leaving quite abruptly. He must have been on the lookout for someone else for the night to calm his libido.

Thong, who walked out too, chatting with him in Thai, came back to tell me that Chon was ready for paid sex, some ₹1000, since it was no longer a chemistry of top and bottom, no longer about preferred roles. Without seeking my opinion, the offer had already been turned down, and Chon had walked out of the Soi.

Heaven knows I would have paid!

SIX

SEX, LUST, LOVE AND A MASSEUR CALLED NON

It was close to 2:00 a.m. when I left the Telephone Pub, preferring to walk to my hotel, which was a few kilometres away. Walking back at that hour, on that night, helped me absorb and catch the last minutes of Pride and experience the leftover sexual drive of men who were still waiting for a hook-up, a passionate cuddle or maybe even the beginning of a relationship.

There were over a hundred gay men outside DJ Station, getting a late-night meal on the main Silom Road. All of them appeared to be fit and every other person was wearing a sleeveless white T-shirt and blue or white denims. There was this now-or-never aura about them as though you'd never see them again. There was arrogance in their body language too. I thought it came from the power of seduction and the enticement of gorgeousness, or maybe it was just me, weak in the knees, in awe of the abundance of beauty around me.

One of the men pitched himself to me unhesitatingly, saying he was up for grabs, if I were ready to take him. 'My home is too far from here, I can go with you to your hotel or condo,' he made his availability clear. I, however, lacked the courage to respond or start a conversation for no other reason than my own inhibitions.

Although I had somewhat gotten over the overt consciousness I had felt during my first visit to Bangkok, I am most comfortable in structured surroundings where there is some amount of certainty and control—not sure if these are appropriate words though. For example, I had never taken to cruising and was more at ease at bars, restaurants, discos and gay chat sites. I suppose it was that all these places provided a layer of privacy from the world outside. It was also easier to strike a conversation in such spaces, build some form of titillation and expectation through a play of words, something that didn't put sex at the centre of an interaction or make the need for lust and pleasure obvious. I guess obviousness was still a concern then—the obviousness that I wanted sex. And even though I had opened up to one-night stands, the honest admission of the pleasure of sex and the desire to have it continued to linger somewhere in my head as a shallow act, a sin and that I was of poor character. Quite obviously, I still thought I would be judged or was judging myself, as it couldn't have been the Thais or anyone on that street.

So, I walked on and away, heading towards my hotel, disappointed with my hesitancy, going back empty-handed in a city where tourists, old and young alike, usually had someone by their side. It was so common that the receptionist looked over my shoulder and beyond at the sliding entry door to the hotel, assuming I had company. 'Are you alone?' she asked me, the intonation making it amply clear that it was a statement and not a question.

Once in my room, I decided to indulge myself. As I filled the bathtub with warm water, relaxing salts and bath gel, I rummaged through the bunch of gay guides and brochures that Wayne had shared with me during my first visit to the city. I found several 24-hour genuine massage spas providing an outcall service. The word 'genuine' implied authenticity—that the masseurs were qualified—as opposed to sex massages where there weren't any benchmarks such as degrees or certifications. I picked the Banana Spa, since it had good reviews for hygiene standards and technique of their masseurs. It was also gay-friendly.

Till midnight, the spa gave online customers the option to pick their masseur from a gallery of photos. This choice was offered at the spa, too, where men would line up before the customer like it were a show window of a retail store. I told the executive who took my call it didn't matter who they sent, as all I wanted was a good massage to relieve the fatigue from my body.

In about 20 minutes, there was someone knocking at the door. I quickly covered myself in a bathrobe, still not fully dry after the dip in the tub. On opening the door, I found a fair, young man, with a slightly longish face, bigger eyes than most Thais I had seen, a sparse stubble of a moustache, a near-V-shaped jawline, a hint of a goatee and just around five feet and five inches in height. He was wearing tight white pants, a sleeveless lemon T-shirt, which revealed his muscular arms that seemed to be the results of a daily workout. His smile beamed like a ray of hope, 'I am Non, can I come in to give you a massage?'

As you'd guess, I was delighted to see him. I was charmed by his pleasant persona, friendly nature, politeness and his restrained beauty. 'You call for a very late massage,' he commented. Feeling guilty, I apologized, aware that it was now close to 3:00 a.m. 'Mai pen rai, I will take a quick shower now. Have you showered?' he asked. It was a hygiene practice of most Thai masseurs to bathe if they visited your hotel or home to give you an oil massage, as that involved body contact through their bare hands, arms and elbows. They would also request customers to take a bath if they hadn't already.

Since I had just stepped out of the tub, I waited for Non, sitting on one side of the bed, still cloaked in the bathrobe. On coming out from the bathroom wearing a white towel, tied firmly just below the navel, he turned off most of the lights to create a spa-like ambience. The dim lighting turned the image of his body into a chiaroscuro painting, with firm upright nipples and abs—my idea of desire and pleasure.

He instructed me to lie down on my stomach and take off the gown. He gently stretched over me to adjust the pillow, to avoid any strain on my neck and shoulders. Soon, I realized how competent Non was as a masseur, as his firm hands knew exactly where the nerve points were and how the meridians ran from the feet to the shoulders and to the neck. He was gentle and certain, checking if the pressure of the massage was appropriate and if there were any parts of my body in pain and in need of greater attention.

This was my first outcall massage ever. This was also one of the best experiences I had—feeling calm and relaxed in the comfort of the hotel room and in the capable hands of Non. As he started massaging my lower back and upwards towards the shoulders, I felt something touch and tickle my anal cleft or what is called the crack of the butt. The light caress and sensation repeated itself in an almost rhythmic manner, in tune with his coordinated hand and body movement, swaying up and down my back.

At first, I thought his towel was touching my butt. But when I moved my hand curiously to try and feel what it was, I realized it was his penis, and it wasn't limp! I wasn't aware until now that Non had taken off his underwear and was in the nude below the towel. I was incredibly livened, aroused, not knowing what other surprises were in store for me that night. Non, however, was unmoved by my discovery of his ramrod, working diligently, gliding his hands perfectly along my back, between my legs, reminding me of what I had missed—the touch of a man.

It was time for me to lie on my back, revealing my hairy chest and stomach as well as the aroused state I was in. As the hour ended, the now most beautiful-looking man was on top of me, and then I was over him, as we indulged in passionate moments of intimacy, not once looking at the time on the clock or realizing that the morning was not too far. We both lay in bed, staring at the ceiling, extremely pleased, relieved and slightly connected. 'It is too late for you to go home. You can be here tonight,' I offered.

Apparently, not many customers allowed or asked a masseur to stay over, unless there was an agreement for a 'full service, full night' package. Such agreements were usually negotiated in advance with the spa. The cost of extra services, though, such as penetrative sex, were all left to the masseur and customer to determine on the go. In our case, there was no such conversation, as it was mutual fun, all very organic, a seamless transition from a massage to sex.

Non stayed over. We woke up around ten in the morning. We showered together, and I ordered breakfast for both of us. 'No one has done this for me. You don't need to,' he said, holding my hand, swinging it like it were his, and I liked that. As I paid him for the massage and added a tip, he looked at me, returned the extra, and posed a question: 'Will you call me when you come back?'

That minute, the world around me ceased to exist, all I could see and feel was him, the softness in his voice, his smile and touch. I wished for our paths to cross, although I was unsure why. Throughout the flight to Delhi, I wondered if it was love, infatuation, the element of surprise, the unexpected sex or sexual chemistry that kept me thinking of him? Or was it everything around me: the city, the freedom, the fullness of life, the surprise elements and him?

On my return to Delhi, I was eager to share my latest experience of Bangkok with my friends. While Pride topped the list, meeting Non was given special attention, and the few photos of his saved on my laptop were lapped up with relish. Before I could get into any details about him, my friends collectively called him boyfriend material—a snappy conclusion. 'Just look at his smile, his face structure. He is so sexy, hot—anyone would want him as a boyfriend,' exclaimed Rahul. There were no two views on that, just a conclusion that he was 'the one'—he fitted the look of a guy I ought to be with.

While I was pleasantly surprised by the instant approval for Non, I felt we were like one of those families picking girls for their boys, and in some cases boys for their girls, for an eventual nuptial. I was reminded how parents and their parents, aunts and uncles would sift through photographs, trying to adjudge a person's character and nature from their 'looks', which seemed to decide who is beautiful, vicious, joyous, pleasant, loving and even sanskari and marriageable.

In a jocular manner, I said, 'Geez, you guys approving a man for me based on a photograph is like a traditional marriage set-up!' Rahul slapped me on the back and retorted, 'Oh, come on, it's human, we all do this.' And in a more serious tone, he said, 'It isn't uncommon to respond to a face, a picture, what attracts us, or to have a love-at-first-sight moment. We all have an eye for certain features and details.' But, as another one of my friends, Mohit, said, although there was innocence in our responses, there were external influences on how we defined beauty and attraction—'How do you explain the obsession with *gori chitty*, fair and lovely?'

Appearance, however, is important in the field that Non was part of. He invested greatly in his fitness, meaning the shape of his body. He also spent time tending to his eyebrows, eyelashes and lips. While these features added to what we called vanity, the emphasis on his skin was significant. He had over a dozen cosmetics, including lotions, face packs, serums, face and body washes and whiteners. This kept him going and glowing in the market, competitive enough to face the younger lot who'd enter the business every year. 'It is not only about my skills as a masseur or ability to satiate a customer,' he had told me, 'as clients usually see my pictures before hiring me.'

As I listened to him, I could hear the challenges girls faced in the marriage market if they were aged, while the age of a man and his marriageability was rarely in question. I thought of models in the world of fashion and advertising who had a short shelf life, women actors who lost their relevance and ranking once they became mother's and air hostesses who didn't just fight unruly passengers but also the ageing process.

I must admit ashamedly that I was as discriminatory as the market. And I am not referring only to the age factor that I spoke of earlier when Pop and I met. I preferred a certain body structure, what we call a 'type'. I was attracted to slim men, the waif-look, and those who were usually referred to as 'Oriental' looking. I liked youthful boys. I liked those who had little hair on their body or face, preferably none, a category that the community call 'twinks'.

At times, I wondered why and what lured me towards the younger lot—was it a flaw or a problem—only to be reassured by a psychologist that it wasn't merely a queer thing. 'It isn't unusual,' she said, confirming that even heterosexual men were attracted to far younger women, and many women liked much older men. 'Societal norms for wedlock rule out huge age gaps, so we don't see or hear about it normally,' I was told.

Still, I'd tell myself that after I came out at the age of 30, I was emotionally inexperienced and young, probably searching for my missed years in the youthfulness of others. And Non was everything that fitted my type!

With his photo being a conversation starter amongst my friends, there were a number of typical questions: What does he do?; Where is he from?; 'What is his education?; and 'How did you meet?'

Non, I replied, wasn't an urban boy as such, not from Bangkok. He belonged to Roi Et or Isan, one of the Thai provinces in the central north-eastern part of the kingdom, sitting in the foothills of the Phu Phan Mountain range. He had moved to Bangkok to earn money, just like many other Thai boys looking out for themselves, paying for their education fees and saving to send some money home. After graduation, he had studied massage therapy at the respected Wat Po Temple in the capital, where locals and foreigners trained, learnt the history of the skill, healing and how to serve.

It is from there on that I chose to spin a lie. I had concealed how we met and what extra services he offered as a masseur.

I claimed that he gave me a massage at a top-end spa in Siam Square and that we decided to meet later over drinks to celebrate Pride. There was a reason why I did this.

While there were youngsters like the newly-weds I had overheard during my coral reef tour in Pattaya, there were enough and more people, gay men too, who carried a conservative and sometimes religious view that sex work was immoral, a sign of social decay. There was also an assumption that sex workers were bereft of the emotions to have feelings for someone. It was believed that those who took currency for sex could do anything for money, as they had no values, at times trapping clients in their maya jaal or honey trap!

I, as it were, carried no such impression or rigid thought, as I believed everyone had a heart and the potential to love, irrespective of their profession. My view was that even ruthless money-makers, hate-mongering politicians and people who had the license to kill or had killed someone had a 'soft' side to them. Of course, I was aware that power and money could control people, and many marriages were arranged around bank balances and assets, yet I was convinced that everyone could love. That my friends Pop and Non did so in the most liberating way, where the body was never treated as a possession or the only factor that made love tick.

Although my friends weren't terribly enthusiastic about Non's line of work, a masseur, suggesting I call him a therapist, a slightly more respectful description for his line of work, they were excited about seeing him in real life. They were also keen to have an authentic Thai meal, cooked by a Thai, which Non had committed to before he boarded his flight to Delhi.

What I needed to do was stock up my kitchen with Thai condiments and sauces, noodles, pork, seafood and chicken, and a lot more fruits than we regularly consumed (for his four-hourly snack). I also had to sketch out an itinerary, covering tourist sites and restaurants that he should visit. At the top of the list, though, was the urgent need to replace my slim single bed with a larger queen-size one so that he and I could sleep together the way we had in Bangkok.

All in all, I wanted Non to feel at home, to make my home his!

SEVEN

NON IN DELHI

Non's welcome to Delhi was what most tourists experienced: a mix of shock and awe.

He was in absolute disbelief seeing the worn-out state of the puny airport, which I told him was the second-busiest terminal in India then. Hoping to see cafés, restaurants and an abundance of retail, he was disappointed to find the airport housing a nondescript, poorly stocked duty-free outlet, which he walked through in less than a minute. In search of water, he located perhaps the only eatery in the terminal and was astonished to find it in the shape of a kiosk, with its corners bandaged in red and black tape.

The wobbly cart and the creaking baggage belt aside, what made his arrival less than welcome were the intrusive in-your-face taxi drivers hawking their services, out-shouting each other, leaving him visibly petrified. 'I can't tell you how happy I am to see you,' Non exclaimed, relieved to spot my face amidst the chaos. The relief, however, was short-lived.

As we drove into the city, the blaring horns and the zigzagging drive left him unnerved. He was used to the peak-hour traffic congestion in Bangkok and dodgy tuk-tuks but not what he witnessed in Delhi. And then there were the cows that he gasped incredulously at, wondering how they were allowed to park themselves comfortably on pavements, roads and dividers. 'This because the cow is a sacred animal, isn't it?' he asked hesitatingly, unsure if it was disrespectful to pose such a question, given that religion and religious beliefs were both personal and political.

'I think so,' I shrugged, saying that Delhi was a divided house when it came to Gau Mata. Many agreed cows on the streets were a traffic hazard and a risk to life. There were others, I confirmed, die-hard worshippers, against displacing the animal from its chosen abode, recognizing its personal choice as sacred. 'A choice you don't have, and a cow does,' he remarked under his breath, making a point that hadn't crossed my mind earlier.

Non was a curious sort, keen to walk the streets, explore local food, markets and religious places, and observe how we lived. We ventured in all directions, visiting tombs, mosques, temples, gurdwaras and churches, giving him a flavour of what we called 'secular'. The sheer mix of architecture, aesthetics, quiet and soul of the different religious spaces overwhelmed him. So did the variety of Indian cuisines he tasted at several restaurants, as did the experience of handicrafts from different states he saw at Dilli Haat. And there was good reason, as till now he had assumed Hinduism and Hindi would be central to the capital city, that butter chicken, dal makhani, chicken kebab and naan roti was what all Indians ate.

He even thought there was a singular structure and palate of colours for Hindu temples, expecting to see a replica of the one on Silom Road. He didn't expect a Birla Temple constructed in white marble or the expansive and distinctive Akshardham, which had been just a few months old at the time. 'Most Buddhist temples look alike,' he said, drawing a distinction, a homogeneity he was familiar with.

The city's green cover and the many parks he saw enamoured him. He liked the fact that pretty much all public transport had moved to CNG, and we had an efficient yet small metro rail system that was considered green. Additionally, it was the low-lying skyline, as opposed to the Manhattan-like structures of Bangkok, that caught his fancy.

As it turned out, these were amongst the reasons Non liked our home, a two-floor bungalow, dwarfed and sandwiched between double-the-size residences on either side. He enjoyed the kitchen and the terrace filled with potted plants, creepers and hanging baskets that created a green look, easily identifiable on the busy main road in front of our premises. It delighted him to find lemongrass, kaffir lime, galangal, celery, sweet basil and several other herbs growing in terracotta pots, the results of Ma's hard work and green thumb.

He wished Ma were in town and not away at my eldest brother's home so that he could have cooked for her, and in exchange, learnt about naturopathy and alternative healing that she was proficient in. His way of thanking her for his stay was a gift of a Thai silk stole and a number of recipes, all vegetarian, that he scribbled in a diary, which I still have and refer to.

For me, there was a great sense of joy, returning from work, being welcomed at the door by him, with a Thai meal waiting. The kitchen was spick and span; the table was beautifully laid; and the bed was always ready to sleep in, with puffed pillows and neatly tucked bedsheets. If I were tired and aching after a long day at work, he would use his skills as a masseur to ease me of pain and stress. And when we had my friends over, he was quite the co-host, in and out of the kitchen with me, conversing with everyone and, like what Ma and I usually did, was the last to serve himself.

In those few days of growing familiarity, I thought Non had settled in, that we were on our way to creating a sacred space for ourselves. 'Your friends are warm. Your collection of music, the art on the walls, it is all so appealing,' he said earnestly while lying in bed after lunch, the day before he was to return to Bangkok. 'But there is something missing in this city,' he said after a moment's reflection, unable to put his finger on it in a definitive way. In an effort aimed at specificity, Non retraced his short visit, enumerating certain incidents and characteristics that struck him as strange or different from his experience in his own country.

He recounted how he saw well-off people bargain combatively with street vendors who were struggling to eke out a living. 'This makes the poor, poorer,' he observed. He was stunned by remorseless customers yelling at waiters, as though it was a right that came with the power of money. He felt it was thoughtlessness that permitted minors to sell newspapers and magazines at traffic junctions, when the press itself should have been protecting the rights of children. He found it odd that basic utilities such as lavatories were not accessible to all, and that hygienic options were there only for a few, a certain class of people who visited restaurants and hotels. 'People can't be blamed if they urinate on the streets, against a wall. I can't imagine how hard it must be for women,' he said.

As he continued with firm persistence, now insisting that people stared at him wherever he went, I was hurt. I experienced a pseudo-nationalist moment of my own, ignoring the spoken truth, wishing to counter him with whataboutery. I wanted to remind him of the poverty in Thailand, the high number of drunk driving cases on highways, and that the media was not absolutely free and the nation was overly dependent on foreign tourists—people like me. I, however, backed down before uttering a word, switching sides as they say today, since he swiftly came to what bothered him most, something that irked me too—the life of women and gay men.

He had noticed the negligible number of women at work in restaurants, at the airport or retail outlets, and, of course, the gay community that was conspicuous by its absence. 'I hardly see anyone gay anywhere we've been,' his gaydar, after all, had almost nothing to respond to.

He had observed how girls seemed to group together at bus stops and restaurant tables, staying at a distance from boys and men. He talked about young and old women alike taking a dip in the nearby swimming pool, fully dressed. While this left him amused, he thought there was a cultural or religious compulsion, 'just like the burkini was to some conservative religions and cultures' that repressed women.

This is when I spoke at length, perhaps going beyond what he anticipated, since it was a matter close to home and heart.

'When we moved to Delhi from Kolkata after my father's passing in 1984,' I began, 'my mother packed away sleeveless dresses and kurtas that she wore "freely" until then.' Any clothing that showed skin, even the arm, she was told, was an invitation to men. And being a widow, there was no man to protect her anymore, a reminder that she was on her own.

Even in the 90s, when I was a journalist, the Delhi bureau always had a night drop particularly for women, keeping in mind their safety, I recalled.

'Then, the media must have tried to correct the problem,' Non presumed, recognizing the power it yielded. 'Negative,' I replied, saying not enough had been done, referring to the unchecked rise of sexism depicted in lifestyle pages and Bollywood item songs, commoditizing and objectifying the woman.

I told him how the noodle-strap blouse of actor Mandira Bedi had made more news than her or her colleague's commentary of the Cricket World Cup just three years earlier (2003). Leading English dailies and journals had reduced her presence to sex appeal that stirred up the male hormones. And, like her wardrobe, a top-selling English magazine had written the Indian team had gone through several 'plunges' of 'form'.[5]

At the few dinner parties I hosted during Non's visit, he witnessed single women arriving, neck, chest and arms covered. In minutes, they would remove their light jackets, dupattas and stoles worn like a shawl, since they were inside a safe home. He watched them leave much earlier than men, and in groups, once again, covered up the way they had arrived. Each of these guests were told to message or call me once they reached their destination, 'like it were some underground secret mission,' he hissed and snarled, sounding agitated.

Non, as it were, was aware of class divides and the power of money, as it was part of Thai society too, something he experienced every day being a masseur and sex worker. The divide, though, 'was not as harsh, stark and demeaning,' he said. There were reported cases of rape and molestation as well, but nothing that placed the blame on women or bound them to their homes, denying them basic dignity.

That same evening, we got the horrific news of a three-year-old girl being raped in her home by a neighbour in the National Capital Region (NCR). I remember Non using the Thai words, *khwām xākhāt phyābāth*, which I understood as 'deeper malice', a term often used to describe the normalization of 'men will be men' and 'boys will be boys', suggesting that women are the culprits and need to change or mend their ways!

This news, as it flashed on television and phones, took the

---

[5]'Cricket World Cup 2003: A year of Mandira Bedi's noodle strap, girls, gimmickry', *India Today*, 5 January 2004, https://tinyurl.com/3v34f4v5. Accessed on 20 September 2022.

spirit and joy out of that night—Non's last in Delhi. Hours before leaving, he sat me down at our dining table, looked calmly in my eyes and posed questions: Other than my job, why did my mother and I live in Delhi? If roughly 50 per cent of the population, i.e., women, live in fear, where did the gay community stand? 'We are a tiny minority with no respect here, only *klaw*, *klaw*, *klaw*,' he said, using a Thai word meaning distress, fear and uneasiness.

'To be safe is not the same as to be happy,' he proclaimed, something that most of us had forgotten, especially women who had reconciled with the expectations that society had of them, their space and lives. I had listened to mothers, daughters and sisters appeasing each other and themselves with words such as 'our lot' and 'destiny' to rationalize the lives they led.

And my answer to Non was strangely fraught with denial and submissive: 'This is where my mother and home are. There are ways to get around things, to find happiness. Life is bound to improve!'

As gay men at that point of history perhaps we were guilty of romanticizing our pain, the struggle and the delightful fact that we violated social norms and the law by being gay for a few hours at a club, a home, in bed with a stranger or engaging with anonymous people on a chat site. Maybe, given the privilege that the few of us had of an open home, the choice to travel to a gay-friendly city or to pay for sex, we insulated ourselves from what freedom was or could be for ourselves or others, and what it is to choose and have options. Or possibly, we had normalized a restrictive living, finding solutions within the 'system', which explains, to an extent, my absurd reply.

When I look back, Non's quick study of Delhi was clearly a wise man's work, 11 years ahead of what the Supreme Court articulated in its August 2017 verdict on privacy: 'Life is worth living because of the freedoms, which enable each individual to live life as it should be lived.'[6] Non taking offence with the visible lack of safety for women and gay folks was echoed in the same order, that privacy includes sexual orientation, and 'is not lost or surrendered merely because the individual is in a public place.'

As I saw Non off at the entry gate of the airport for his flight back to Bangkok, his big beaming smile was back. He pulled the luggage trolley to the side, stopped, turned around and hugged me, 'Please don't mind what I said. I care for you and am thankful for your hospitality. I wanted to know how you live and what it is like to live in your city after meeting you in Bangkok, and now, I know.'

I wondered whether he was delighted, upset, disappointed or disillusioned with his short experience of Delhi and where we stood as a couple, if we were one. But what I did know was that he hadn't closed the door on me. Non left with the words, 'I know you will come to Bangkok repeatedly. You deserve it. Come and see me when you do, if you'd like.'

Of course, I was going to return to Thailand several times over, and regardless of his circumspect 'if you'd like', I was

---

[6]Chandrachud, D.Y., 'Justice K.S. Puttaswamy (Retd) ... vs Union of India and Ors. on 24 August, 2017', Indian Kanoon, https://indiankanoon.org/doc/91938676/. Accessed on 20 September 2022.

definitely going to meet him again, as there were so many things about him that had grown on me.

Apart from his physical beauty, which was very much attractive, I found his confidence, acute observations and cutting remarks equally appealing. He was curious by nature, someone who did and would continue to stimulate my mind and intellect. His skills as a masseur were admirable, so was the effortlessness with which he managed the home, including the kitchen and terrace garden.

When I met him again, four months later, he had just moved to a larger room at the deep end of Sukhumvit, having saved up sufficient funds over the past three years. It was a clean, air-conditioned room with an attached toilet. There was a double bed with a thick Dunlop mattress and a spacious cupboard fitted into the wall beside a desk that accommodated books, an electric kettle and cups. He proudly showed me his room, 'It is not the size of your bedroom, but it is my space of calm and joy, enough for me.'

There was everything he wanted or needed a stone's throw away, including laundromats, pharmacies that were open till midnight or after, departmental stores and food kiosks besides the 7-Eleven chain that dotted almost every street in the city. 'This makes life easy for those of us who work long and late hours, not sure if we'd have time to cook or wash our clothes,' he said. Apparently, the multitude of services available to locals and foreigners were all part of the revered King Rama 9's objective of a sufficient economy. 'You really don't need more to be happy,' he uttered, perhaps intentionally, as it relayed back to our last conversations in and about Delhi.

Non was busy with customers at the spa as well as attending to outcalls he received over gay chat apps. We met each other a couple of times at the Telephone Pub, often having hurried interactions, as he ran off to attend to his work engagements, returning to my studio apartment only once, towards the end of my trip. He arrived early, at 6:00 p.m. For some strange reason, we both sat at the edge of the large bed, not saying much. I suppose we knew there was a distance between us or something not quite right. I broke the silence by talking about Delhi, trying to sell a future life, that the city was bound to change, not that I had any basis to pitch such a prospect at that time.

'You don't have to explain anything to me,' he said very softly in a quivering voice, which was followed by a long minute of silence that seemed cold and numbing. 'Non, what is happening?' I asked anxiously, 'What is on your mind?' He got off the bed, sat on his haunches, held my hands in his, looked me in the eye and revealed what he felt: 'I like you, Sharif. You are kind; you care for me. You understand my work. Yet, we are so different!'

Sensing the fragility between the two of us, my eyes turned red, tears trickled down my cheeks, I questioned him, 'How different?' I rattled off bits and pieces of the time we had spent together, the sexual chemistry and his hug, the warmest ever.

'You'd want me to move to your home and city, but to inhabit that city would be living like a prisoner,' he exclaimed. Basically, what he meant was his ideas of equality, choice and freedom were at odds with what he had encountered and noticed in Delhi. 'If you'd live here, we'd stand a chance. You would have me and everything you like about this city,' he offered an option that I couldn't consider then.

Non had tears in his eyes too, yet he was more in control of himself, unlike me. I was shaking, embracing him tightly, holding on to the moments just before he left. Once he did, I remember how my mind vacillated oddly, behaving like I was a victim—first blaming him for letting me down, and then holding his visit to Delhi responsible for the distance that had come between us—in some way denying the plain truths that he had spoken of.

He was right that I ran the risk of falling prey to 'our' culture, as I recall lapsing into a strange mode, wondering why he couldn't 'adjust' to Delhi like I had, after all, in India, to adjust was a sociocultural compulsion of over a billion people. I guess I had forgotten how and why freedom and acceptance was liberating, passing over what drew me to Thailand, a culture that allowed Non to be who he was.

Some 30 or 45 minutes later, however, I came to my senses, respecting his confidence, certitude, wisdom, affection and beauty—all that I admired about him. It didn't make me feel lighter or happier though, as it led to more sobbing, with an indescribable sense of loss washing over me, realizing I had failed in my endeavour to settle down and was not cut out for a relationship. And as they said in the marriage market, I was unsuitable for a very suitable boy.

EIGHT

TO LOVE IS A BATTLE

On the flight back from Bangkok to Delhi, there was an angst simmering within me, but I couldn't identify a specific person or people to be angry at. I recall it being atmospheric. I felt defeated but was out of words to describe the sense of loss. I wanted to cry but my tears seemed to have stopped in their tracks, like they were done, exhausted!

Even though I was complete as a person in a logical way, I felt incomplete, just like what single people were told if they were of a marriageable age, or like me, older, in the mid-30s. I felt irresponsible, a word commonly used for those who hadn't married or sustained one. People close to me knew of my abysmal success rate with lovers—four men in five years, none who stayed beyond a year to a year and a half.

The misery was far worse than what I had undergone when I had flunked twice in school, in class five and six, as even those who failed in schools and universities, the most corrupt of people, rich or poor, had successfully settled down. I, as many would say, had everything going for me: a career, living in a South Delhi home, part of a family that had accepted each of my boyfriends as 'the one'. Thus, every relationship that didn't fructify into a long-term one questioned how I went about connecting and associating with other gay men.

For several nights, I was morose and aloof, wondering whether there was a formula or template to follow that I had missed. I had gone by instinct, and whenever I felt unsure, I turned to romantic stories in books and films for tips. I had even indulged and invested in capitalist tropes, be it heart-shaped chocolates, cushions and cakes, a bouquet of roses or rose petals spread on a bed in a dimly lit room fed by candlelight, or handing a single rose, which was popularly considered 'complete' enough to symbolize love.

Why on earth, I asked myself, was romantic love so slippery, fleeting and momentary? Why was the fullness of hope emptied so easily? Why was my commitment to love, to my partners, so worthless? If there was anything that made me feel better, even a tad bit, it was the fact that I wasn't the only one grappling with these questions, seeking remedies and solutions.

As a community, a legion of gay men had seen men come and go before the seasons changed. Our joys through relationships were so uncertain and brief that some couples celebrated a one-week anniversary of being together, raising the pitch when a relationship was a month old. We would laugh that off, nervously I thought, in our own queer way, calling these milestones the 'joy of small things'!

Many of us took solace in each other's experiences, as we had, sort of, accepted love and heartbreaks, frequently falling for lust instead, protecting our hearts from the vulnerabilities that love had so far provided us. As several psychologists and studies said, and from what I had seen and experienced personally in Thailand, this was a natural option for mental well-being, a means for validation, a counter to depression.

I remember us clinging to songs of hope. Cher's 1998 dance track 'Believe' was huge, telling us that there was 'life after love', that we were 'strong enough', not needing the one that had left us 'anymore'. We flipped and wept over Madonna's 'You'll See' (from a few years earlier), which delved into hurt, hope and break-ups, giving us strength through lines such as this: 'You think that I can't live without your love?/ You'll see'. We even dramatized tracks such as 'Kaanta Laga' and 'Choli Ke Peeche' for their ability to acknowledge instant love or love at first sight and the hidden, throbbing heart, breaking the norm with what they said, a queerness we could relate to.

But even music was momentary, just like booze at a gay party; after all, alcohol can never be a replacement for the thirst water quenched—a perennial need for life.

My search for a boyfriend started days after I came out in August 1999. The first one lived in Delhi's Paharganj area, considered an old part of the city. He 'succumbed' to marriage, not only since it would lead to turmoil within his family had he chosen 'us', but also since he didn't wish for his mother to go through the trauma of knowing her son is gay. He didn't want her or himself to face social oppression either.

The next was a tribal boy, a postgraduate student from a Northeastern state whose family had adopted Christianity. He feared coming out, living in paranoia that tied him down, impacting the relationship we shared. The Church, he had said, would not accept him, he'd be thrown out of his home and worse would happen—his parents would be humiliated and mortified!

Just before Non, I was with a 'working-class' Bengali, as he called himself. In his late 20s, he flew away to Europe in pursuit of sexual freedom, love and safety. He feared being outed at work (a globally renowned outsourcing company in Gurugram) and home, a household that included his sister and widowed mother. 'If I stay back, I'd be finished, and my mother would be devastated,' he had evinced his anxieties.

In all three cases, as you'd guess, the issue wasn't the lack of love. It wasn't about compatibility or, as was said, our inability to tango. It was, as one of my queer friends said much later, in a dry, sardonic way, the dancefloor wasn't ours—a fact that didn't strike me at the time of the break-ups.

I would always take the blame, believing I had wronged, feeling disenchanted and abandoned. Yet, I wondered what my fault was, trying to locate instances where I could have done something differently as though I could turn back time. I would finally slip into periods of despondency and depression, the phase I had been sliding towards when Non and I had parted ways. I'd usually define my mental and emotional state with the words of Mahatma Gandhi—'where there is love, there is life'—as I thought it best described the gloom and darkness I endured. I was unaware, though, that these lines had little or anything to do with romantic love and had a far larger context and meaning, something that had a bearing on all lives, queer ones for sure.

Apparently, Gandhiji was speaking about bonds and bonhomie in society at large, a mass of people and their individual freedom, the liberation that comes with love. According to my middle brother, Dwijen (who we called Duji), the quote meant, 'Each person's right to be free is to freely love, and through love comes life and light, and a beacon for society itself.' For a long period of history, he explained, 'society lacked that kind of love', as we as a nation were and continue to be divided by caste, religion, colour, region, food, language and so much else. 'The seeds of love,' he believed, 'just like charity, have to be sown and nurtured in homes,' by households, letting it power through each division, realizing its ability to unify people.

Duji was a liberal, a believer in 'live and let live', and a diehard propagator of freedom built on the strength of love, peace and humaneness. Hence, when he did speak of the core of Indian families being arranged marriages, reportedly over 90 per cent of nuptials in India, he expressed his displeasure at the death of individual choice but didn't rule out that some matches worked. He said, 'You can't erase a small number even if it were miniscule and not recorded,' a fact that I would have shouted out had I been in the Supreme Court when it re-criminalized homosexuality in December 2013, calling us a 'miniscule minority', not worthy of being counted.

By the same token, my brother didn't wish to ignore hard facts, specifically the prevalence of domestic violence. The last National Crime Records Bureau report I came across claimed that of all the crimes against women, 30 per cent were cases of physical assault in their homes, defined in the law as 'cruelty' inflicted by husbands and their relatives against wives.[7] If we go by a *Mint* report from April 2018, based on data collated by the government-run National Family Health Survey, we'd have to accept that 99 per cent cases of sexual assaults go unreported and that 'the average Indian woman is 17 times more likely to face sexual violence from her husband than from others.'[8]

While some of this data wasn't available when Duji and I had this conversation, I recall him saying grimly, sort of mourning the demise of love and care, 'I don't wish to get into other crimes inflicted on women or children, including mental torture.' Of course, I was aghast and horrified to know that officially over 100 children were sexually abused every day, in and out of homes.

To put things into perspective, Duji handed me a book by Nivedita Menon titled *Seeing Like A Feminist* where she refers

---

[7]Dhawan, Himanshi, 'Not Rape, Domestic Violence is Top Crime Against Women', *The Times of India*, 5 October 2020, https://tinyurl.com/yk6jyspx. Accessed on 11 October 2022.

[8]Bhattacharya, Pramit and Tadit Kundu, '99% Cases of Sexual Assaults Go Unreported, Govt. Data Shows', 24 April 2018, *mint*, https://tinyurl.com/ydwzymjr. Accessed on 22 September 2022.

to a Delhi High Court order of 1984 that said Fundamental Rights had no place in a family. Essentially, 'if every individual in the family is treated as free and equal citizens, that family will collapse.' Meaning, she expounds, 'the institution', as it was designed, 'is based on inequality', perpetuating the hierarchy of age and gender.[9]

Therefore, given the social compulsions of marrying—a duty and dharma to many an individual—I started to believe that for a majority of people, creating a family was automatically prone to being a dispassionate exercise. It was bound to be bereft of heart and respect, where even children were produced out of an obligation rather than love. And children were brought into a world and families where the denouncement of equality and choice was legitimized through examples set at home.

What Duji did was open my mind to the ecosystem we lived in, admittedly, a process that began only after I came out, engaging with the community, activists, lovers, and my experiences in Thailand. In multiple ways, he implied that expecting change of a significant kind, whether social or cultural, in our society and nation was unreal. After all, as Gandhiji opined, 'what is true of families and communities' remains to be 'true of nations', irrespective of what the law is or what a constitution says.

In so many ways, my brother made me realize that our home, or households like ours, were privileged and culturally different from the majority. We were not the kind of family that would stand with and by the Delhi High Court order of

[9]Menon, Nivedita, *Seeing Like A Feminist*, Penguin Books Limited, 2012.

1984. We were a home where my brothers picked their own partners, women they fell in love with. When I came out to my mother, I was gifted a lovely checked shirt, turning the day into an extra special one. That was love too.

To be who we were, I understood, was a deep belief in love, a certain kind of fraternity, a history of acts, actions and convictions that dated back to the 60s, when India was considered less progressive and open than now!

My father, who we called Papa, was smitten by Ma's looks and enamoured by her grace. He had interacted with her at a conference of the Economic Commission for Asia and the Far East (ECAFE) conference at Delhi's Vigyan Bhawan. Papa was there as an economist and futurologist, and Ma was part of the hospitality team, looking after delegates such as my father. He was hell bent on connecting with her, using his network to find out about her family and their coordinates. Succeeding in doing so, he met her parents and unabashedly sought their permission to marry their daughter.

Just 19 years old, my mother was impressed by his courteous, mild-mannered behaviour, youthfulness and stylish French beard. She had never been wooed this way before, nor had someone taken her out for a meal or coffee.

Ma's father, who was fondly called Nanu, found Papa's academic qualifications—a PhD from the London School of Economics—and friendliness as plus points. Her mother—called Mom by our generation—liked him but thought he was presumptuous and forward to have come home and proposed, instead of his parents. Least bothered, Nanu waved her comment off, recognizing my father's sense of independence and values, seeing in it his decisiveness towards Ma and matrimony, and his pro-people ideology.

In contrast, Ma wasn't the studious kind, rarely read books and was hardly keen on a career, holding on to a part-time job with an airline, hoping to fly the world one day. When passing out of school, Ma told her father that he could send her to college if he had money to waste but harbour no expectations of her being scholarly. Nanu wasn't upset. Notwithstanding their austere lifestyle, he cheered her on, encouraging her to follow her passion for dance, sports and the arts.

With such an upbringing, what we'd call broad-minded and liberal in today's parlance and politics, it was only natural for my mother to have the last word on her marriage.

Ma considered several things before saying yes. To start with, she was aware that those days, everyone had to marry 'no matter how free you are'! Then, Papa's presence was pleasant, 'nice to be around'. He was also appreciated by her parents. These thoughts notwithstanding, what tipped her towards a relatively quick decision was Nanu's health. He had leukaemia. 'If I could give him a little joy, a wedding in the family, then why not?' she recalled, demonstrating what, I believe, was the importance her father and family held for her.

Although this wasn't the perfect definition of a love marriage, Papa's family called it so, contrasting it with marriages that were 'fixed' by parents. It was also a union between two different castes—my mother is a Kshatriya (also known as Khatri) and my father was a Brahmin. In Hindu varnas or social classes, it is said that both these castes are 'pure' and 'upper caste', carrying virtues and choices that are unavailable to others.

Be that as it may, a Brahmin is known to stay within their own, which is why there was some amount of discomfiture in my father's family about Ma's (lower) caste. They also raised questions on her being a Delhi girl, distant from their way of living, not a Marathi. My father—being the only son of five children, treasured and doted on—may well have used his male advantage, choosing love, standing his ground, getting his parents to bless his union to my mother in the year 1961. He even moved out of the family home, starting his married life miles away, protecting and creating his own culture of an open home, the kind we treasure to date.

I remember my Aaji (paternal grandmother) saying Papa turned out to be rebellious, having gone against convention and their family. She attributed his belligerence to the English education he had obtained in a Mumbai college and further studies in London. I understood from this that to her, and similar people, to choose a partner, to proclaim one's love, were foreign imports, not part of the Indian psyche or culture at that time. When Aaji tied the knot in the early 1900s, she wasn't an adult, had no say and was literally married off, an orchestrated matrimony, by her parents. This is how things were then and were supposed to be in the 60s and decades to come, she said.

Irrespective of her complaints and grumbling, Aaji grew to be very fond of my mother. She admired the fact that Ma learnt the only language she spoke, Marathi, ensuring the two could communicate comfortably, reducing the possibility of misunderstandings. She relished Ma's adoption of Marathi cuisine too and how she looked after her during her stays with us. Clearly, with the passage of time, Aaji's inhibitions about my mother's caste, the region she belonged to and being an outsider of sorts, vanished. In fact, according to Papa, she called out for my mother in her last hours, showing how fond she had grown of Ma.

Ma started out in the Rangnekar family clueless of what it was to be married, what she'd do as a wife. Her main focus was keeping the pack together and giving each of us room and space to grow. 'I enjoyed running the house,' she would say, it wasn't a subjugation at all, it was a preference over a career.

Yet, when crisis hit us, when we ran low on cash and savings in the late 80s after Papa's demise, Ma doubled up as the primary bread-earner, working as a professional alternative healer, turning her free service of naturopathy, acupressure and reiki into a partly paid consultancy. She only levied a fee to those who could afford to pay. For almost a year, what she brought home was our main source of income.

What she learnt in alternative healing was the salience of the five elements—air, water, earth, space and fire—that govern the world around us and combine in different forms within our physical beings, referred to as doshas (body constitutional types) in Ayurveda. If the balance of proportions is lost, it disturbs the world and troubles our physiology. To her, this equilibrium, an ideal, was an ecosystem important for peace, calm and love to flourish. I suppose this approach to life made it a little easier for her to accept and learn about homosexuality.

Like most parents of a certain time and conditioning, 'we only knew about man and woman, their weddings, unions and friendships,' she said, almost apologetic for not knowing about gayness in the way she knew healing. Through conversations, she realized how we as a community had been banished from the varied world of people and sexuality. In spite of her support, Ma became cautious about people in general, what they'd say, how they'd respond and whether being open about my sexuality was wise or a danger. Even when I had a boyfriend, she'd rather keep it a secret, introducing him as a friend.

I guess her trepidations and hesitation were founded in her own lived experience of family and society. First, it was finding her way into Papa's family. Then, and far worse, were our early days in Delhi in 1984 when, at the young age of 43, she learnt what it was to be a widow.

Overnight, Ma's wardrobe had gone from colourful to white, like there was only a single dimension to who she was. While wearing sleeveless outfits was blasphemy (as I had told Non), the dupatta that she wrapped stylishly around her neck now covered her head, much like a hijab. Her instinct for art was ignored if not destroyed, probably since it was a form of freedom, an extension of oneself, an expression. In a way, Ma lost her voice, even if she denies it, as every piece of work—faces and body forms—were packed away, placed in a loft, not visible to the eye and too high to reach.

If this wasn't enough, she faced questions on her character, as we had several male visitors, colleagues and friends of my father, coming home to pay condolences, offering help if we needed any, particularly paperwork. And these barbs and questions came from people not too distant from us, they were those who had otherwise cared for our well-being.

Not a single person thought of the pain and shock Ma must have undergone. There was no semblance of sensitivity towards her or intelligence to understand that the field Papa had belonged to—journalism—was male-dominated and had a tiny number of women, a skewed sex ratio at work that families and society itself had fostered.

Those weeks, months and years were a complete contradiction to the life she had led when Papa was around—a full life, where she had been an artist, designed and stitched her own clothes, modelled for magazines and been a member of the Censor Board of Film Certification. She choreographed dance sequences for some of the biggest theatrical productions of Mumbai, was a presenter of radio programmes and also worked part-time as a copy editor for an advertising agency. Ma was happy hosting dinners with my father, meeting journalists, filmmakers, musicians and academics, and being part of similar functions held elsewhere. And as a family, we were all part of this and a lot more!

When asked why she had not retaliated or protested against the treatment meted out to her, she replied, 'I preferred silence, not wanting anything to take me away from my priority'—of bringing us up, her three boys—'what else could be more important?' Ma said she picked her battles, not fighting everything that was a botheration, and had no regrets!

Ma's approach to life was a lot like her first cousin, Sheila

Masi, the former chief minister of Delhi. When Masi was to marry Vinod Dikshit, who had proposed to her in a Delhi Transport Corporation (DTC) bus during their university days, the nuptial was delayed by around two years. Masi, like Ma, was obviously a Khatri, whereas 'Vinod's family were Brahmins!' Masi shared. It was Amma, Vinod Mausa's mother, who didn't favour inter-caste marriages, not his father, Uma Shankar Dikshit, who we called Dadda. Eventually, however, it was the patience of 'Dadda, Vinod and I that wore Amma out,' Masi told me, leading her to give up and give in to the love between Mausa and Masi over an arranged marriage for her son that she had earlier preferred!

Soon after their wedding, Masi went to Dadda's home in the Nazarbagh area of Lucknow, where she had a first-hand experience of an entirely different culture. Dadda had forewarned her that 'we are rooted in tradition'. She spent three days hiding her face under a ghoonghat and 'cooking for what seemed like an unending procession of relatives' she said. Not just that, she slept on the floor in a tiny, dingy room with utensils all around—'it was a different era' Masi explained. Some would define her experience as demeaning towards women, Masi, however, lodged no complaint, only telling Vinod Mausa how alien the experience was, knowing full well that the love and understanding they shared was far more important.

When I knew of this history and its slight parallels with Ma's, I saw in it a reflection of a generation or households that took everything as 'normal' and in their stride. I also wondered whether their way was an example of negotiating life and its various situations, the skill to prioritize and have the ability to see life beyond oneself. Or was it love, love for those who mattered most, that helped them power through the challenges they faced? Perhaps it was all of the above, but I would want to put love at the top!

Ma and Masi lost their husbands at a young age and immediately focussed on their children. 'I had to be strong for them,' Masi wrote in her autobiography, *Citizen Delhi: My Times, My Life*, grieving in private just like Ma did. But this is where the similarities in their lives ended. Being a politician, she had an active public life that Dadda encouraged her to continue, knowing full well it was a panacea for pain. Ma, as it were, had to wait till Mom came around, which she did, bringing a spring back to her life.

Probably carrying the burden of guilt that my mother had been wronged, Mom insisted that the whites be put away or dyed to different colours, providing no explanation for a change in mind. She also encouraged Ma to step out of the home, which she did, albeit cautiously, taking 'unquestionable' decisions, attending classes on the Gita, Vedas and Upanishads and completing a course on child welfare at the National Institute of Public Cooperation and Child Development (NIPCCID). She studied alternative medicine and obtained degrees in naturopathy and acupressure, studies that my eldest brother, Dilip (whose pet name was Dipu), motivated her to pursue, knowing that she had always wanted to be Florence Nightingale.

Within the four walls, however, she was quite confused, unclear of how to 'behave' as a single parent. 'I didn't know what it meant to "wear the pants" in the house and when to change into a salwar kameez,' she said. So, she went about things instinctively, being strict, bold, sometimes angry, but also friendly, loving and motherly. In so many ways, this dilemma and spontaneity could be described as fluidity, an unrelatable equation with gender norms, or, as some called it, being Ardhanareshwar!

When Dipu and Duji grew from boys to men, our home transformed back to an open house, a lot like how it had been when Papa had been around. It was normal to find the kitchen with 15–20 plates piled on top of each other, at least thrice a week, waiting for 'friends of the boys' who would drop in for lunch or dinner. It wasn't unusual to find girls as part of these groups, sometimes outnumbering the men. Some of them, as it happened, were special to my brothers, girlfriends they were dating or the one to wed.

At the age of 24, Dipu decided who and when to marry. Duji, when he crossed 26, did the same. There were murmurs and chatter amongst certain relatives, suggesting that Ma had abdicated her responsibility by 'allowing' my brothers to do as they wished, meaning selecting their wives. There were questions on whether she had met the families of the girls before giving her approval, whether she had sussed them out and figured out their economic and cultural backgrounds, as some asked: 'Are they at the same level as you or our family?'

For all practical purposes, Ma was thrown a rule book of norms, a list of checks and balances and equations, the ones that a few relatives alleged I had ignored in my search for a boyfriend and partner. She, nevertheless, stood her ground, 'It is their life, they are adults, I am there to bless them,' holding on to what seemed to be the same thread that Papa had held.

Once my brothers moved on with their lives and purposes, it was I who had the privilege of calling over colleagues and later my world of mostly gay folks, contributing aggressively to what our home became—a safe haven for people like me!

Ma was so involved in the creation of this world—ours—that she seemed lost, a definite misfit in a local senior citizen's group that people connected with at their age. She looked visibly bored and tired at a meeting held at home, over tea, pakodas and samosas, coming to the kitchen, saying, 'I don't know what to talk to them about!' Whoever struck a conversation that evening, spoke about their family, narrations that were least delightful. They found flaws in their daughters-in-law's abilities to cook. They disliked their desire to work or that they were working already and 'neglecting' the home. They complainted about the clothes worn by women, and that the younger generation was reluctant to adhere to sanskars, falling in love, showing no regard for family, caste, religion and class!

Ma, as it were, had seen and heard enough of this over the years, something she could not subscribe to or indulge in any longer.

With the open house we had, she let herself grow in directions she had never envisaged, using vocabulary that was several generations apart and younger than those of her age. She was comfortable talking about 'consent' with my pals, understanding the right over one's body and the relevance of #MeToo, not deriding those who claimed they had been violated by senior male colleagues just because they spoke up years later. She talked about happiness as a need and right for each individual. She listened intently to the love stories and attractions of my gay friends, egging them on to go for it. She understood the healing of the mind, as much as how time helps in the process and that it isn't always easy to offload baggage that has been placed on one's shoulders as a compulsion of 'time-tested' systems, the normative.

And I learnt that it was the normative that perturbed her the most, not for herself (anymore) but for me.

There was a worry she carried, something she grasped years after I came out to her—it was that I was an outsider to the world and its social order. And that I had been and was at a far greater risk than she had been as an outsider to our family and a widow in society, where her being a woman and a wife, chosen by Papa at least fell within the gender binaries of society and matrimony.

So, as I understood it, the open house we had, became more about me and her gift to my living, the making of a protective zone, where no one could harm me. It was a neutralization and correction of sorts of the external world that she partook in as well, of love lost and gained. It was queer in its own way, as it was about chosen people—the ones we chose and the ones who chose us—what the queer community called a chosen family.

One of my closest friends said our home was an oasis. She explained it as a counterculture or sub-culture, where the spirit and energy of diversity allowed love to stitch bonds between disparate individuals through common human values. No wonder then, our first-floor residence became a place where you could be anyone and be yourself, where love and lovers were welcomed, no matter who you loved. In more ways than one, as Helmer said after his few visits to Delhi, we had invoked the Thai cultural philosophy of mai pen rai.

But I was so absorbed in our bubble-like home, I forgot that the world beyond our threshold was where my ex-boyfriends lived and future ones would come from, what Non called a 'prison'. I had even forgotten that the broad line and the polarized world between the outside (what people would say and expected) and the inside (what we felt and breathed) was never going to be easy to dilute, whether young or old, something I had experienced, in one way or another, since my pre-teens!

NINE

THE NAME OF THE GAME

As children we were taught a number of things aimed to prepare us for social engagement—people visiting our home and when we stepped out. It was about behaviour, temper management, recreation, the importance of education and awareness, personal hygiene, consumption of food, music, television and films.

We learnt about table manners—how to use a fork, knife and teaspoon, and how to eat with our hands. We were told about why the elbow should not be on the dining table, why we should not stretch across to pick up a dish, as it could obstruct the person sitting next to you. We learnt that closing our mouth while chewing was not only about manners or that it sounded terrible to some ears but was also about the air going into the stomach, causing gas and indigestion.

The ideal way of eating, Ma told me, was to sit cross-legged on the floor or on a chair and eat off the plate. Called padmasana in yoga, this position is said to enhance the blood circulation in our body, while the act of bending over ensures the stomach muscles work efficiently, helping with the digestion, keeping the tummy tight, usually putting a limit to the portion of a meal. I also learnt about the banana leaf and its scientific role when food is placed on it, how it helps retain moisture and nutrients in a natural way, something that stainless steel plates and crockery could never do.

But in the world beyond the four walls of our home and in the presence of others, sitting on the floor or cross-legged, eating with the hand and off a banana leaf was labelled and presented as a symbol of poverty and backwardness. Which is why, I guess, even when it was just us having a meal in the dining room, Ma would sit cross-legged at the table in an obscure manner so that we didn't pick up a habit that depreciated our value in society. It was only when we grew up, habituated with the customary codes of behaviour, did we see Ma sitting comfortably in padmasana or a vajrasana position (which is even healthier) while having a meal, as we sat on chairs at a table, accustomed with the physical and social elevation it gave us.

As kids, when we stepped out to play games—cricket and kabaddi being my favourite—we took collective decisions determined by the majority. We would huddle in a circle, place our hands in the middle, one over the other, with our palms facing down. We would then release our hands in a coordinated manner, leaving every individual with the choice of showing their palms or knuckles. After a quick count, it would be decided whether the palms or knuckles won or lost. Though innocent and above suspicion, this was perhaps our first learnings of majority over minority. And what we weren't taught was how this could play out in real life.

Most parents of a certain class didn't think of educating us on equity, equality and majoritarianism, or how a democracy should function. They must have thought schooling would take care of this through classes on history, literature and political science. But I don't remember the problems of majoritarianism being drilled into our heads through day-to-day examples, or for that matter, what it is to be a minority.

The closest we got to any such topic, I suppose, was when Papa and Ma would remind us that India is a poor nation, so we must share, be polite and generous. Papa had once told me, 'Don't seek power, pelf and prestige, you already have enough,' which I understand today as advantages, access to a system or what is commonly called privilege.

In an article from 1982 that my father wrote for the *Business Standard* titled the 'Ritual of Remembering Gandhi', he said that Gandhi rejected the philosophy of the 'greatest good of the greatest number'.[10] The reason, and I quote, was 'it meant that in order to achieve the supposed good of 51 per cent, the interests of 49 per cent were to be sacrificed.' I was too young when this article was published and my father passed away long before I read it, denying me the opportunity to discuss

[10]Rangrekar, D.K., *The Politics Of Poverty: Planning India's Development*, Sage Publications, 2012.

the nuances of what he wrote. Duji, however, explained this in simple terms—that being a minority should not mean being a slave to the majority.

At home, as it were, we were handed down clothes and books, shared stationary and toys, and had a few outfits that were stitched from a single thaan. Ma tried to make sure our individual preferences in food were catered to through the week. This was one way to get us to taste what each of us liked. She also believed that the three of us were very different. To her, bringing up children was the same as being a gardener—ensuring each plant was treated individually, giving them shade, sunlight, water, soil and manure as per their requirement.

Ultimately, though, Mom (my grandmother I spoke of earlier) believed that no matter what we learnt or practised at home or school, we all had to 'make a name' for ourselves. '*Naam kamana hain*,' only then would society accept me, she had said. Moreover, I had to work hard and never forget to respect my father's name, part of my duty to the family, she insisted, setting ground rules to follow.

Mom came from a generation where education was a privilege meant largely for boys, a majority of whom were admitted to schools that taught in English. While she was lucky to make it to a Hindi-medium school for a few years, she learnt to read and write English almost entirely on her own, becoming an ardent student of western literature, always searching for Mills & Boon, Perry Mason and the Sherlock Holmes series. The compulsion to learn the language, however, was an external imposition, as she was made to feel less than everyone else in a world where the language commanded prestige and respect.

Nanu, of course, had educational credentials that got him a good job at Greaves Cotton. He engaged with a qualified set of managers and engineers, British and Indian. Whenever there was a social function, although she placed delicious food on the table, Mom felt left out, trying hard to get a word in, in Hindi and broken English, often feeling or made to feel embarrassed. However, when she learnt the language of the Raj and conversed with senior officials, it benefited her and Nanu too, as it added to his prestige and name.

Given her hard-earned joy in reading and speaking English and my disinterest in studies and a career, I would quote William Shakespeare: 'What's in a name? That which we call a rose, by any other name would smell as sweet.' But she rejected this reference outright, without any clear explanation, saying, '*Yeh sab kitabi baatian hain* (These are bookish statements),' the real world is something else, and she had witnessed and lived it to say so!

Still, on umpteen occasions, I enjoyed reproducing this very popular and profound line from Shakespeare's *Romeo and Juliet*, disrobing the importance of a name, giving weightage to the worth and meaning of a person instead. So, if Romeo had another name, Juliet would still have loved him. Some say Shakespeare was way ahead of his time. Some argue that this is what sections of the Vedas say, as it dismisses the physicality of a being: shape, size, names, caste, class, political boundaries and identities. They are all meaningless, a veneer.

But to answer the question 'What's in a name?' and what

Mom meant, I realized there was much to it.

My full name, as you must have read, is Sharif Dinanath Rangnekar. The first name has always left friends and strangers alike wondering if I were a Muslim. On countless occasions, I have been asked in a suspicious, and sometimes apologetic, tone, 'Mohammedan?'

To my Hindi teacher in Kolkata's St. Paul's School, the name was an insult to the Maratha leader Shivaji. 'How could a Maratha have a Muslim name?' he lamented, less concerned about my inability to structure a proper sentence in Hindi. He called me Sajjan, a Sanskrit word meaning noble, and used a pencil to write it over my name in the class register. I had to follow him, scribbling Sajjan on my note and textbooks.

In 2002, my first name even caused panic to a family friend and lawyer, Daniel Latifi. As the Godhra riots captured the news headlines, he rushed from his residence in the neighbouring Niti Bagh, beads of sweat running down his face, panting, as he said, 'Change your name immediately.' His reason—the riots might spread to Delhi, and if this happens, 'fundamentalist Hindus may bay for your blood'. And Muslims, he exclaimed, could be as violent, assuming I was a product of an inter-religious marriage, and therefore disloyal to Islam and its claimed and proclaimed practices!

A little over a decade later, an immigration officer at the T3, Delhi airport spent over 10 minutes trying to understand how my title came to be. He was aware that Rangnekar is like Tendulkar—Marathi. But how did Dinanath, a 'pure word', which meant God or *dukhiyo ka sahayak* (helper of the downtrodden), sit with a Muslim name. He was evidently unaware of the Egyptian actor Omar Sharif, who I was named after, as his only connection was the Pakistani political leader and former prime minister, Nawaz Sharif. I feared an Islamophobic reaction; however, he surprised and relieved me of my momentary anxiety with his belief that Sharif, Dinanath and Rangnekar strung together reflected a borderless world, secularism and unity, putting it into the context of changing politics, not 1968, when I was born.

Around the time I became the chairman of the consultancy, the senior journalist, the late T.V.R. Shenoy, provided me with a social Hindu context. 'Do you know you are a Gaud Saraswat Brahmin—a GSB?' he asked. I was flummoxed. I learnt then that I belonged to a special group of Brahmins tracing a direct lineage from the Indo-Aryans that spread through the coastal areas of Maharashtra, Karnataka and Kerala. According to Mr Shenoy, as a GSB, I should hold my chin up, my shoulders back and chest out, and 'walk with pride'.

Hardly did he know that 'pride' had an altogether different meaning for me—a rise up against homophobic heterosexuals, not a 'look down' structure of caste that placed people like me at the top of the pile with advantages.

Ironically, when I started my career at Penguin Books, I was handed the task of proofreading *The Penguin Book of Hindu Names*, written by the politician Maneka Gandhi. At that time, I was oblivious of the fact that such a book would have a market, but it went on to be a bestseller, going into multiple reprints. It had become a handbook for many a namkaran (naming ceremony), an important ceremony to innumerable Hindu parents wishing to give their newborn child an appropriate name.

Across religions, I understood, names were derived from gods and goddesses, virtues, values and morals, positive elements of nature, from father's and mother's names as well the place of birth, amongst other things. An aunt had once claimed that the selection of a name was aimed at shaping a child's mind and character, giving them a meaning, a value and a moral to live by.

Yet, I was not fully convinced about how this played out in real life. For example, a friend of mine, Sushil, was expected to be of good character or virtuous, as his name suggested. Poor chap, he was never allowed a drop of alcohol until he got married; he was 26 when he tied the knot. When in school and even university, he was not permitted to express his opinion at home and had to follow a strict regime of studies and minimal recreation. This discipline, he told me, was how his parents felt he'd be a man of good character—sushil!

While Sushil's situation was true of many parent–children equations, I wonder how his parent's names had shaped their character and behaviour? I recall us joking that if Hitler was a gender-neutral name, it would fit the profile of several parents, teachers, bosses and politicians—who probably used their names for deception, knowing how blind people are to rituals of naming. But who would question this aspect and fact in a nation where we are so often asked, 'What is your good name?' A suggestion that all names are good and equal!

When I entered journalism after the one-year stint in

publishing, I had to live up to my father's reputation or naam. He was known as a futurologist, economist and was a revered editor and a friendly chap. Once I established my credentials as a reporter, first with *The Pioneer* and then *The Economic Times*, several senior journalists attributed my instinct for news and prolific reporting to my DNA. There were a few who claimed that I had lived up to being a Rangnekar, a Brahmin, as I seemed to have 'that' kind of intellect.

When I switched lines and moved into the field of communications and PR, I carried with me the genetics of a credible journalist. There was an expectation within the industry that I would deliver high-quality work, as I understood the psyche of a reporter and how the media worked—a key component in the outreach mix for a brand or corporation then. My journalist friends, however, presumed I would use my crusader approach in reporting, to run a broom through the PR business that had been suffering from a trust deficit those days.

I, of course, had more pressing deliverables as the CEO of the then little firm—to build its name and make myself visible in the market, to bring in business.

When I entered this field, it was close to 14 years since India had opened its economy to foreign investment and adopted neoliberalism. It was a fiscal year that saw GDP grow at 7.5 per cent, despite, as the media said, a 0.7 per cent growth in agriculture[11], suggesting India was less reliant on the farm sector and more modern and industrialized. The nature

[11]'Economy Grew 7.5% in 2004-5', *Business Standard*, 25 February 2013, https://tinyurl.com/4wrwyyhu. Accessed on 25 September 2022.

of neoliberalism was competitiveness of products, brands and people, all playing in a marketplace, making it a perfect foil for a society obsessed with and defined by a one-upmanship and '*log kya kahenge* (what will people say)'. It was ideal for the business of PR, too, for the same reason as much as it was for the media, driving consumerism as well as lifestyles that scripted the pecking order of hierarchies.

Yet, given that India had witnessed jobless growth for over a decade, it was obvious that wealth and power were distributed in a not-so-equal way. The reasons were apparent: the relationship between caste and class, the resultant access to a system, the name you carried, the names you could drop and the people you were connected with.

Owing to business imperatives and the role I held at the PR firm, I had to crack and infiltrate a circuit of very elite people, the rich and famous of Delhi, who were at the top of the social echelon, the crème de la crème. Most of them resided in the southern and central parts of the city—Sunder Nagar and Lutyens'—now referred to as the 'Khan Market gang'. It was an interesting clique that called themselves liberals, 'free people'. Yet, they generally assessed a person by their public profile, residential address, net worth, the set of wheels they drove, attire, pronunciation and enunciation of the English language and knowledge of fashion, wine, cheese, whisky and politics.

Apparently, I ticked a few of these boxes, which afforded me a pass. It was the position I held—a CEO. I had a chauffeur-driven car, access to certain senior editors (power), and lived in a home built on a 500 square yard plot located on what was an emerging arterial road of South Delhi. One criterion without the other, I ascertained, may never have given me entry into the 'club', as once I moved away from the corporate world, I was more or less a faceless, nameless person, holding an irrelevant address, falling off their map!

My experience, mind you, wasn't unique to me. It was something many experienced. Why, even the well-known author, journalist and political commentator Dr Sanjaya Baru recalls that at one point he was an outsider, but 'as an editor at the Times Group and someone who knew Prime Minister Narasimha Rao well,' he was 'welcomed into the charmed circle of the Lutyens' elite.' Once he entered the prime minister's office, as the press advisor to Dr Manmohan Singh, just about every door opened for him and every club had his name on it as a member, VIP and special guest. But the moment he resigned from his role with the then PM, all of this vanished immediately, what he calls a 'reminder of my revised status'.

Baru, as it were, was part of a sprinkling of intellectuals, mostly senior journalists and academics, who were invited to cocktails and dinners hosted in that area of Delhi. They were often hand-picked, I was told—the ones in the know of scams, government policy or were proximate to certain members of Parliament, members of Legislative Assembly, politicians, corporate honchos and ministers. It was easy to spot them, as they usually donned shirts and kurtas made of khadi or regular cotton, a Nehru jacket and traditional footwear from the states of Rajasthan, Gujarat and Maharashtra. There were exceptions, of course, a few who were least interested in what they wore (shirt not tucked in, trousers that were dated, be it colour or style), more invested, as they were, in intellectual stimulation—mind over matter.

Other than this set of people, there was a smattering of gay men, usually seen with the most fashionable women at the parties. In fact, it appeared, the community was sort of the 'in thing', the happening newbies. I often felt we were somewhere between a discovery and a fashion accessory, being introduced to everyone by hosts with, 'Look, this is my friend, and he is gay and a darling. Isn't he nice?'

It turned out that we were a symbol of liberalism. Our presence added to the image of this group, breaking away from wealth and stature that they were known for, to having a humane side, 'a cause', which their sophistication didn't allow them to rebel for in the way human rights were addressed—on the streets and in the open. Gayness also brought to the party a certain coolness of being different, of being a Rock Hudson or George Michael, a western connection that appeared more modern and ahead of where (the rest of) India was.

Parties such as these and people such as us appealed to the new crop of lifestyle reporters too, populating what was called the 'Page 3 culture'. As it happened, a number of gay fashion designers at these get-togethers featured in one article or the other, queering column centimetres through photos and words, presenting us as trendy and fashionable. Although this changed the depiction and representation of the gay community from the earlier and continuing homophobic reports in the city pages, we got associated with the upper class, stinking rich and a socially unacceptable western way of life and culture, obliterating our history of belonging to our own nation.

No wonder, the label of being an 'import', smuggled in, sneaking through the 'customs' of our country, stuck to us for a very long time. And this was the same lens used against women who chose to drink, hold a cigarette between their fingers or wear short skirts and low-cut tops, talking about sex and pleasure—deviations and practices that were not part of our sabhyata or culture.

I was a silent spectator then—naïve, ignorant and voiceless. I wasn't open and out about my sexuality then, sharing my secret with only a few.

I was cautioned by a dear friend and former colleague, the late Arindam Sengupta, the editor of *The Times of India*, about coming out and carrying my sexuality on my sleeve even in these groups. He said that the corporate world, the rich and elite, loving as they may be, were conservative and proponents of freedom only to publics in a very pictorial way, an imagery of a lifestyle, of hugging and friendly smiles, as though everything is okay and everyone is equal. But these actions were usually superficial.

As per Dr Baru's account, once the parties ended and the guests left, all their liberalism would disappear. Behind closed doors, in most cases, they'd be marrying off their children within their caste, judging and gossiping about the lives of others, deciding who's in and who's out, who's okay and who isn't. And that 'other' could have been me! Which is why Arindam's deepest worry for me was this: 'Your name in the market, the credibility earned, could all be destroyed in minutes, the moment they know you are gay.' It would take nothing to destabilize my career, my status in society or in family, he had said, admitting that these were generalizations about a group of people but possibilities and realities too.

There were several attempts to malign me. First, it was someone hacking my Hotmail account, just when I had quit *The Economic Times*, sharing an email I had exchanged with my brothers of my first-ever cruising attempt at an ice-cream parlour with other gay friends. Next, was the invasion of my laptop, which had gone for servicing, where queer content from it was made available to some officials working with companies associated with the consultancy I headed. Then came a constructed campaign over text messages, asking colleagues across levels to disobey their CEO, me, as I was half a man, and suggesting they should collectively see me out.

I came out of these situations, somehow, going through anxiety and panic attacks. But this was indicative of what fears the community in general carried. An international report (covering India) from Accenture says only 14 per cent of LGBTQIA+ people felt fully supported when it came to being welcomed. And only 31 per cent of the community surveyed was fully open, irrespective of their talent, skills and competence.[12]

So then, what's in a name if there is no meaning to the worth of a person or a community? How do you 'make a name' if the depictions of who you are, are not written by yourself and are

---

[12]Accenture, *Visible Growth; Invisible Fears Getting to Equal 2020: Pride*, 2020, https://tinyurl.com/nhcbcdwd. Accessed on 25 September 2022.

skewed and appropriated by other people's biased narratives?

I wish Mom was alive—I could then narrate to her these issues, my love life and my life in Thailand. I would tell her that as part of a cultural tradition, Thais are given nicknames at the time of birth, sometimes even before their official name is registered. These aren't pet names, as they are used inside a home and outside—not to shape one's minds, character or something to live up to.

I would share with her who Non was, and that his name meant 'sleep' in his language. He didn't measure up to it, he didn't need to. He was awake, hard-working, skilled, practical and wise. I would tell her that Pop was a mere nickname too. He didn't seek to be pop or popular. He was everything alternative, where his idea of liberalism came from experience and the self. That freedom, to him, was aptly about personal choice, not a definition, a label or a pictorial display of consumerism, wealth and power.

I would have written long letters to her, describing in detail how Bangkok was, how valuable its space was to me, why Telephone Pub was not just a bar or pub; it was a hub that spoke to my soul. I would have even informed her that friendships and love have different meanings, that they come in different forms and equations. And as I had witnessed in Thailand, there is no shame in exploring them, and no one should ideally tread with fear in doing so!

TEN

OH FEAR, WHAT CAN THE MATTER BE

On every occasion I travelled to Bangkok, even if it were an official trip, I would go through a near metamorphosis within myself, feeling relaxed, smiling like the welcoming cabin crew on a Thai Airways flight. The tiredness in my shoulders or the stiffness in my neck would vanish into thin air as if I had left these aches and pains back in Delhi. I would breathe better, sleep well, even if it were for fewer hours than I normally did. Even if I consumed more meat, oil and chilli, unlike my veggie-centric, low-oil and low-spice diet at home, my tummy never revolted, and the irritable bowel syndrome I usually suffered from, would disappear!

While I was always fastidious about the quality of sound emitting through an amplifier and accompanying speakers, I was happy with a small, nondescript Bluetooth dock, playing music from my phone. I was content with a handful of shirts and T-shirts, pants and a single pair of shoes, as against a wardrobe of clothes and over two dozen distinctly styled, multicoloured footwear. And even if the hotel room was tiny, much smaller than my bedroom, I would feel least constrained, quite pleased, like it were my home, a precious little world of mine. All in all, I seemed to have more energy, more grit and a lot more stamina, feeling at ease.

On any given day, I could grab a coffee at a 'gay' café or a 'mainstream' one, finding a mix of sexualities in both. I would run my fingers through piles of queer books at a 'regular' bookstore, buy queer-designed products at large 'conventional' departmental stores, cruise at mid-market to upmarket food courts, on the BTS Skytrain and at my hotel lobby, elevator and gym too.

Whenever I came back to Delhi, albeit with regret, I was told I looked fresher, fitter and had a glow on my face, as though I had been through a body-cleansing detox. I would look relaxed, smile a lot more and sometimes fold my hands to greet someone, like they did in the country of smiles, forgetting how important the handshake was to urban Indian culture. I would tell friends, family and colleagues that the smile and namaste were part of a lovely culture and to not attribute it to a bygone tradition or politicians seeking votes.

But who'd listen, when, according to one of my senior colleagues, a firm handshake was an attribute of masculinity and modernity, a namaste was for women. This was one of many rude reminders that I was back in Delhi, other than the morning doorbell of our old house help, who would occasionally remind me that I must get a bahu for my mother!

Delhi was growing into a modern urban centre with large streets, an efficient metro, the revival of arts and culture, an expanding green cover and a young set of people who seemed interested in exploring a new way of life. The city, however, had a heightened reputation of being the 'rape capital', an unsafe place for women. Which is why, I guess, the firm handshake of skin touching skin was better off being a man-to-man thing, and the namaste limited to women, who, incidentally, could hug other woman as a means of greeting.

On my return from these trips, I would habitually 'report back' to my dearest friends Chitra and Venu, sometimes, with Thai goodies in tow and many new stories to tell. Chitra being the lady she is, would notice a number of things, not just the 'glow' of my skin. She'd say there was a change in the tone of my voice, suggesting I sounded more confident and chirpier. She pointed out on numerous occasions that my shoulders were straighter, unlike the slouchy bent that would return in a week or two after my break. Even my gait appeared firmer, she would observe.

According to her, I was going through a psychological and physiological change on every trip to Bangkok; it was an emotional journey from worry and anxiety in Delhi to an unfettered way of life in Thailand! It was only when some of my gay friends made their first trips and repeated visits to the Thai capital that Chitra's observations assumed greater meaning and context. 'You could be gay anywhere and at any hour, there is space for us everywhere,' said a friend, encapsulating my unbridled emancipation in a land far away from home.

Ironically, it was on a flight to Thailand that I happened to re-read Rabindranath Tagore's 'Where the Mind Is Without Fear', written over 120 years ago. It was a poem I was familiar with, as it was part of our school curriculum. My lack of worldly wisdom and innocent understanding as a youngster, though, had left me with a simple comprehension that we should all be honest, knowledgeable and free, holding our heads high, not bowing in shame and fear.

As an adult, I had greater capacity to appreciate the power of Tagore's poem, that the context and setting was the people's struggle to rid themselves of the British rule from the subcontinent. It was about freedom, the basic need for dignity for every Indian as much as it was about the evils of society and the necessity to clean them out, gently, I would assume, given the grace with which Tagore had expressed himself.

The poem 'continues to exhort people – particularly in conflict zones across the world – to seek fearless truth, progressive thoughts and actions,' said Dr Badrul Hassan, a recipient of the Pablo Neruda Prize for poetry, in a write-up for the *Reader's Digest* May 2020 issue. It was a 'hymn for all mankind', he claimed.[13] And I couldn't agree more.

I saw the conflict zones defined by gender binaries and roles, ideologies of the Left and Right, majority versus minority,

---

[13] 'A Hymn for All Mankind: Where the Mind Is Without Fear', *Reader's Digest*, 8 May 2020, https://tinyurl.com/2fwrvh2n. Accessed on 25 September 2022.

mainstream as opposed to 'other' streams and the ability not to be limited by these divisions and tunnel visions of 'either or'. I read the poem as an invocation for a life without trepidation, dread and distress that is experienced by most queer people, caused by an unrelenting heteronormativity and homophobia, which bear similarities with the British Raj ruling over minds and souls, robbing its subjects of their identity and sense of self.

If Tagore was alive, I believe, he would rue the state of our country, the progress of our citizens and the evolution of minds. He would probably see (as he wrote) how the 'depths of truth' are as lost as the 'stream of reason'; all that he hoped a nation and its people would want and must have when free of the clutches of the Raj, a 'heaven of freedom'.

As children we read a fair bit about the independence movement. I listened to stories from relatives, on what the Partition had been like. I learnt that the day we got independence had been a solemn affair in most homes, given the loss of people and property many had incurred along the way, something we seemed to have forgotten when we celebrated the reading down of Section 377—'our' day of freedom.

According to Sheila Masi, families, 'ours included', had opened their residences to homeless relatives and friends, as it had been a way to 'embrace each other's problems'. It had been the 'done thing' in times of a collective or individual crisis.' It had also been how the freedom movement had functioned, she said, where those opposed to the British had kept their home open to mutineers and revolutionaries, unflinchingly.

I have often wondered what it took to be a freedom fighter,

part of a movement for independence, or what it is to be fearless, to hold one's head high against all forms of oppression. I tried to imagine what the British Raj must have been like, an unelected government.

As luck would have it, I was blessed to meet Dadda, who was a freedom fighter. During a conversation in 1987, when I was 19 years old, he shared how he had abandoned his studies at my age, joining the Congress as a city committee secretary. Those days, he said, singing Bismil's 'Sarfaroshi Ki Tamanna', Iqbal's 'Saare Jahan Se Achcha' and Bankim's 'Vande Mataram', had been weapons of expression against the Raj. He had been imprisoned four times, the first being in December 1921, for nearly three years, having taken part in the non-cooperation movement. He had slept several nights in long and large sewage pipes on the streets and gutters of Bombay, hiding from the British sepoys. His body had suffered a great deal of pain and ill health from time to time due to lathicharges, the lack of funds for food and medicine, as he had travelled from the north to west regularly. He had given up, unintentionally though, his responsibilities towards his wife and children, helping others secure their lives as part of the freedom struggle. But, as he said, 'That we could finally have our own elected government, nothing else mattered.'

Freedom fighters, he explained, had been part of an underbelly in British India, where they—a unified force cutting across religions and regions—could discuss their choices, indulge in their own culture and history while imagining a free nation. These dark and dingy places, he told me, had been hidden, known to a select few, as it had also been where strategies had been developed and networks had been built.

When I asked what it had felt like being ruled by the British, he said, 'To be "ruled" by anyone is to create fear, to humiliate and dehumanize the people of a land.' I asked him about the fear he and others must have experienced. This was the only moment I found Dadda struggling to reply, looking up at the ceiling, probably recollecting the terror and frights of those times—I think I touched a raw nerve!

With half a smile, he came back to our conversation, looked through his thick-rimmed black spectacles and equally thick lenses, and said: *'aapko samaj hee nahin aayega…woh samay, woh dar…ek zindagi bina gaurav, bina izzat…yeh chota mota dar nahi tha, usse sehan aur zahan karna mushkil hain* (you will not understand…those days…the fear…a life without pride, without respect…it was no ordinary fear, it is difficult to explain and was difficult to endure)!'

While Dadda could have said a lot more, an elaborate explanation would have still left me with little understanding of his 'dar' and diminished 'izzat' and those days of struggle under the Raj. I didn't belong to his time and was not fighting any sort of power then, to be able to claim to empathize at any level with his struggles as a freedom fighter.

However, several years later, once I had identified as gay, I grew to know how difficult it is to express what fear is, what it is to be denied respect and honour, the anxiety of a lurking danger and a system that is against you. While any such narration would revive wounds, as it did for me even in my

50s, I learnt that no vocabulary, however expansive, was close enough to the lived experience of a minority. Which is why my every effort to explain nervousness, depression and the impact of homophobia to most heterosexuals was often lost on them.

Yet, as some friends said, we could draw parallels with Dadda's life as a freedom fighter and come close, not too close, to what he may have endured. That many of us lived without gaurav and izzat was a fact. That we had to create our own little underbelly and a few spaces here and there to feel free—to talk, to have fun and to work on a movement for equal rights and equity—as if we were in the pre-1947 era too.

The difference, though, as we all knew, was we were living in an independent India and were up against our very own people, parents and kin included, seeking freedom, not independence. We didn't wish to leave our country just because we sought a place for ourselves. We didn't want to be thrown out of our nation as well, just because our idea of life differed with the majority or that we saw much more in the Constitution than was 'given' to us. We were averse to being called foreign or seditious just because our idea of India and being Indian wasn't mainstream or of the majority.

We agreed that every person who came out was a freedom fighter, just by showing their defiance to the normative, the prevailing system. In the context of the movement, as Harvey Milk, America's first openly gay man to be elected to public office in California, said, it added to numbers and to safety. As a friend once said, it was like wearing a badge of pride, honour or bravery! But this was also when a number of challenges came forth, much like the natural conflict between rivers and man-made embankments and dams that aim to control the path, flow and growth of water, contesting the beauty of fluidity.

After coming out in 1999, it occurred to me that coming out itself was a process of learning to engage with people, places and circumstances. I had to use my gut feeling to pick people who I thought would treasure my secret. I had to know when to be free and when to keep my guard up. It was like finding the trusted few amongst a large majority of 'traitors'. My safe spots then were at home, in my bedroom, at Venu and Chitra's residence, at Arindam and Swati's, and with my childhood friend Nitin and his wife, Rachna. I would glimmer with gayness when hanging out with queer friends, burst into colours at home get-togethers, and at the few parties hosted for us in and around the NCR.

Even in the mid-2000s when I started visiting Thailand, successful single men, aged 30 and above were often the target of gossip and suspicion of being gay, unable to marry a woman, something Arindam had warned me about. While the word 'unable' implied an incompleteness in our manhood, many of us chose to ignore the hateful barbs, focussing on ways to fortify ourselves, at least in our places of work. It was sort of the same art of negotiating situations or picking battles that Ma had spoken about.

While there was no 'one' way of being gay, I censored my gay humour or sexual innuendos, curtailed my hand movements, tried to hide any known giveaway of being a homosexual, such as a distinct tone and rhythm in my voice that seemed to be a little 'lady-like'. I kept my attire quite bland, as colours were usually attributed to gay flamboyance, and wore a sleeveless Nehru jacket over cotton shirts, my only form of protest, that too against a suit-and-tie corporate culture inherited from the Raj. I also acted oblivious of any occasional conversations amongst my colleagues on the gay community. I even laughed at homophobic jokes and let occasional humour that reeked of sexism pass; after all, that was a commonly accepted attribute of being a man.

In a way, I chose to do what many Indians did when they moved to first-world countries like UK and the US, adopting the local food, culture, mannerisms, attitudes and accent, to become part of the clique and the power structure, expecting greater security and acceptance. This is also what traitors did, colluding with the British to obtain control, becoming one of them rather than being oneself. A closer-to-home example to why I did this came from the Dalit author Yashica Dutt, who told *The Guardian* that as a journalist, she eschewed 'politics for fear that in writing a story or expressing an opinion she might reveal her caste.' She says, and I quote: 'The fear of being "outed"(as a Dalit) was a permanent cloud, if people knew, would they even sit next to me?'[14]

While a number of my young colleagues got to know of my sexuality, it took me till I was a little over 45 years old, nearly a decade of leading the firm with several accolades in the

---

[14]Dhillon, Amrit, 'Coming Out as Dalit: How One Indian Author Finally Embraced Her Identity', *The Guardian*, 19 February 2020, https://tinyurl.com/46nf3bdb. Accessed on 25 September 2022.

bag, to come out to my chairman, who had always treated me like his son and family. All he said was, 'Don't worry, buddy!' Maybe I could have done this earlier, but then it was he who I reported to, the power above, and as Arindam had said, 'Corporate culture and society are one and the same.'

The problem was that most of us felt compelled to put on an act and hide, internalizing a form of reprisal, absorbing the heteronormative culture that encircles us from birth onwards. It wasn't unusual then or even now, therefore, for some gay men to look at themselves and life from a heterosexual lens rather than a queer one.

Helmer, for example, was unable to accept open relationships, questioning the veracity and love a couple had for each other, calling them immoral. He couldn't comprehend my brief no-strings-attached friendship with a Thai man called Ton, that we weren't boyfriends in the way boyfriends were meant to be. He was uncomfortable around effeminate boys and men, particularly those who powdered their face, used eye shadow and lipstick. He disliked anyone who's hands moved much more than a man. Tight clothes revealing hard nipples, low-cut T-shirts and shorts, figure-hugging trousers and pants displaying the contours of private parts—all were a big no-no. He'd even get angry with street vendors selling gay porn, sex toys and Viagra.

A friend of his, a Danish lady who had spent over a decade in Thailand as against half as many by Helmer, said he had come from a tiny village dominated by the Church and had grown up with its dismissiveness of homosexuals. Further, there was a long-standing belief that gay teachers could 'turn' their students into homosexuals by their sheer presence. While Helmer took time to be more comfortable in his skin, benefiting from the Thai way, it isn't unusual to hear such stories in Delhi even now or across several parts of India.

There were a number of lines of work that attracted ill-informed reactions and homophobia: that a gay doctor, nurse or counsellor would 'convert' and sexually assault young, male heterosexual patients. The situation was such, I was told by a friend, that 'if a heterosexual male doctor preyed on his female patient, the chances of hushing that up were greater compared to a person "appearing" gay, setting off "malicious" rumour mills, enough to destroy his career!' And since such rumour mills were real possibilities and occured in general, daily life too, it wasn't unusual for some of us to seek 'straight acting' men rather than being caught out with a queer femme person who was obviously gay to the straight eye. Yes, some of us were guilty of discrimination against our own!

I recall an incident at a restaurant in South Delhi, a dinner with two gay friends, back in 2005. An over six-feet tall, well-built, Italian friend from the community invited himself to our table. Just about all eyes in that restaurant focussed on him as he moved towards us. He was wearing a black fishnet T-shirt, kajal-lined eyes, nail paint and a colourful pyjama pant, the kind where you could see his private parts dangling. As he moved his hips—in the way women were assumed and expected to—and comfortably queered fashion at that moment, probably enjoying the attention he was getting, we shrunk in our seats, uncomfortable, awkward, fearing his presence at our table would out us. I think I froze for a moment as I saw one of my schoolmates sitting at another table, staring at me. Perhaps I even acted like I didn't know this queer man, receiving him with none of the hugs we usually indulged in when welcoming people from the rainbow spectrum.

We heard hushed voices and loud whispers, a mix of homophobic taunts and wraths, where even our parenting was questioned. Ashamed, we didn't return to the restaurant for over three years, hoping that night was erased from everyone's memory, and their likely conclusion about our sexuality, forgotten.

Still, life was relatively much easier for a cis-gender man such as me. I identified with my given and assigned gender. Unlike a queer femme person, I didn't feel womanly, nor did I desire make-up such as eyeshadow, lipstick and other cosmetics that ladies usually wore. I wasn't apparently effeminate either. However, for those that were 'queeny', campy and effeminate, it was impossible to avoid drawing attention towards themselves or hide their identities.

One of my dearest friends, a queer femme puppeteer, Varun Narain, was subject to bullying throughout his schooling for being woman-like. Heterosexual boys would corner him during recess, in the toilet, on the school field and in the bus to and from home. They'd feel him up, terrify him. 'It was power play, of showing their manliness,' he said. 'I wanted to die so many times,' he told me, saying how much he hated his school days. Varun grew into a recluse, living mostly in his room and the attached garden, using puppetry and theatre to define his sexuality, courageously putting on shows in 'safe' parts of India and the world. With a mixed feeling of relief and ire, he said, 'I would have ended my life without my art and the spine that my mother is!'

Sumit Sadawarti, my much younger pal and singer–songwriter, had almost given up on living when he was 13. While he had a series of breakdowns, he had an ice-cold equation with his father, who he dreaded deeply. He saw him as an alpha male, an expected threat to homosexuality, who detested Sumit's unmanly choice of studying liberal arts at Ashoka University. As it happened, Sumit found some kind of liberation in his studies and at the university. For years, he assumed his life would carry the brilliance and pathos of singers such as Amy Winehouse, Janis Joplin and Jim Morrison, who died of drug abuse long before they knew what it is to be in the 30s. While I admired his choice of artists and their music, his dark thoughts always made me concerned and protective towards him, as I knew too many friends who had cut short their lives—the only act of control they had.

His coming out moment was at a TEDxGateway talk in Mumbai back in 2017, where he invoked Nina Simone's 'Feeling Good', an iconic tribute to the civil rights movement in the US. But that one song and several performances that followed, didn't kill his fear, as so often the desire to live seemed weaker than the want to die!

This terrifying out-of-place feeling was not limited to gay men and queer femme folks. Lesbian women who appeared butch and didn't like dolling up were taunted and told to 'look like a woman'. Some of them were raped by parents and relatives in an effort to convert them to heterosexuality, a truth, as I said earlier, that hasn't gone away yet. Smruti Jalpur, another of my singer-songwriter friends, told me that when she moved to Delhi, bars and restaurants asked her to replace her pant and shirt with skirts and dresses. They told her to be a woman—grow her hair, reveal her cleavage, put rouge on her cheeks, kajal on her eyes, lipstick on her lips and paint her nails! Why? Men drank more if they saw a woman looking like a woman on stage, an acceptable norm. *Aise hi hota hain*! (It is what it is).

Certain global reports find that people from the queer community are at two to six times greater risk of mental health problems, caused largely by the fear of hate, isolation and homophobia imposed by society. Some private Indian research say that over half of the gay community has considered suicide at least once in their lives.[15] And if we deluded ourselves to believe that the world has changed dramatically after the reading down of Section 377, an August 2021 survey conducted by the online LGBTQIA+ community 'Yes, We Exist', says of the

[15]Bentley, Leann, 'Why Does the LGBTQIA+ Community Suffer from Poor Mental Health at Higher Rates?', *Health*, University of Utah, 7 July 2021, https://tinyurl.com/2yrc2uc8. Accessed on 25 September 2022; 'What to Know About Sexual Orientation and Mental Health in Youth', *Medical News Today*, https://tinyurl.com/2tnr2ykr. Accessed on 25 September 2022; 'Diversity & Health Equity Education: Lesbian, Gay, Bisexual, Transgender and Queer/Questioning', American Psychiatric Association, https://tinyurl.com/ysu6kcwv. Accessed on 25 September 2022.

1,700 folks polled, 75 per cent are 'afraid that they might face verbal or physical abuse' if they lived freely.[16]

The only measure of loss due to homophobia in India, however, is stated through economics in a 2014 report of the World Bank, which estimated the cost of homophobia in India at 0.1 to 1.7 per cent of the GDP. That is anywhere between USD 1.9 and 30.8 billion![17]

Ideally, these findings should have been headlining print and television news at that point, leading to debates and editorials on mental health and the queer community, but it didn't. Some reporters told me the topic wasn't important enough, 'Who cares about phobias, mental health or homosexuality in India?' True, but in a year that Indians were looking for change, 'vikas' and 'ache din', shouldn't the economic loss to the nation have been worth a discussion, correcting the wrongs of the past governments?

Of course, I was expecting too much and had forgotten what our family physician, Dr A.J.S. Juneja, had said when I came out to him in 2012. Indian families in general were reticent, unable to understand homosexuality, homophobia, intimidation, the pain it inflicted or that diversity itself suggested there wasn't one normal, he had explained. In fact, as society

---

[16]Jeet, 'Why 88% of India's LGBTQIA++ Community Wish They Were Not Born Here', Youth Ki Awaaz, 16 August 2021, https://tinyurl.com/5cdyk53y. Accessed on 25 September 2022.

[17]Lee Badgett, M.V., *The Economic Cost of Homophobia & the Exclusion of LGBT People: A Case Study*, The World Bank and Sexual Minorities and Development (SOGI), February 2014, https://tinyurl.com/jyebcc8t. Accessed on 25 September 2022.

we have internalized abuse to such an extent that the silencing of voices in homes by the man of the house, is normal. The emotional impact on children, young adults or wives is never considered, nor is the detrimental effect of domestic violence on mental health, an inequity and inequality that the Delhi High Court vocalized and ratified in 1984.

No wonder, when I talked about the glares, glances and piercing gazes that followed us in every public place and space, it wasn't uncommon for some straight people to claim it was an Indian habit; we weren't the target. 'Indians stare at dwarfs, fat people, black people and women in skimpy outfits,' a lady had said in a group discussion, defining a norm that somehow was considered okay.

I learnt that several families where parents remarkably accepted their child's alternative sexuality, would do something remarkably ridiculous too, insisting on keeping it a secret, placing it in a family closet. Their reason was shame—the perennial fear of 'what would society say?' What they failed to see was that the child now knew that their parents didn't have their back once they stepped out of home! Similarly, monied parents were ready to pack off their gay children to faraway lands so that any account of their child's queerness would be erased from their 'local' world. I guess exporting the 'problem' was their solution.

A large number of my friends argued that even if we had the allegiance of family and friends, 'their lens continues to be theirs, not ours', as everything around them normalizes their life and would continue to do so. No wonder, on World

Daughter's Day, a loving WhatsApp message I received has a father asking his daughter if she would love her husband more than him. The question was ridiculous to say the least, but the assumption that she would have a husband erased us. It struck out the possibility of the daughter having a girlfriend, choosing to be single or being transgender, not identifying with her 'assigned' gender.

With such a life, many queer people then (and even today), sort of continue to be freedom fighters like Dadda was. We play hide and seek with the system, winning a skirmish here and there, engaging, on a daily basis, with the conflict zones Tagore referred to. We also hope, as Sheila Masi had said, that those in solidarity would keep their homes open to us, wanting to be part of the 'good fight', genuinely embracing us.

As a mental health expert said to me, living in Delhi, 'we are like pieces of cloth torn in different places,' knowing full well that some of us could run out of threads to hem the damage.

I, as it were, would run off to Bangkok, drape myself in one piece of gayness, torn only by the prospects of returning to the roles and boxes that society confined us to in my homeland.

ELEVEN

'M'POWER

The Delhi High Court order of July 2009 decriminalizing homosexuality was one of the first instances that I felt things could and would change in India, particularly the city I lived in. I believed, like many others, it would reduce the trepidations and anxieties that had become a part of us. I recall the various messages that went around amongst us, congratulating each other, with some quoting from the order, believing, as it were, that our time had come. Sections of the younger generation actually thought so, coming out, tasting legitimacy early in their years and wishing to savour it.

The verdict, from the two-member bench of Justice A.P. Shah and Justice S. Murlidhar, had brilliance written all over it. What struck me with pleasure, though, were these parts: 'It cannot be forgotten that discrimination is the antithesis of equality and that it is the recognition of equality which will foster dignity of every individual.' And then, 'In our view Indian Constitutional Law does not permit the statutory criminal law to be held captive by the popular misconception of who the LGBTs (lesbian gay bisexual transgender) are.'[18]

While quite a few of us read the word 'dignity' for what it is—respect—we also saw it as the creation of a valid space for ourselves, for self-fulfilment. However, the idea that 'what is a popular belief can't be or become the law' was most cogent, as it meant no one had to conform or fall in line with what the majority followed or believed. No social norm can be imposed on people or become a legal stricture. It also meant that the backing of size and numbers can't be a reason to create and enforce laws, that might isn't right, that what is popular isn't necessarily good, right or the best.

Even as we were euphoric and hopeful, my friend, historian and gay activist, Saleem Kidwai, was cautiously optimistic. The doing away of a Victorian-era law, he said, could not resurrect our lives automatically. 'The history of us queer people has been erased from records and thus from our collective memory,' he said, which meant, 'without a history, and therefore, without memory', we as a community were and are 'rootless, alienated and disempowered'.

Further, since the recorded presence of the community has been usually random, arbitrary and often prejudicial, hate against us has been accepted as normal. So, even while the court

[18]Srivastava, Mihir, 'Homosexuality is Not a Crime!' *India Today*, 2 July 2009, https://tinyurl.com/pshdnck3. Accessed on 25 September 2022.

said that 'popular misconceptions' could not hold criminal laws 'captive', we still had the misconceptions to battle, to release ourselves from the captivity of gender stereotypes.

As it turned out, within days of the order, the United Progressive Alliance (UPA) government, which had initially indicated that it wasn't averse to the order, finally chose ambivalence, responding to religious groups who were opposed to homosexuality. The Christian, Muslim and Hindu groups were in opposition. What was most disheartening, though, was the reaction from Girija Vyas, the then chairperson of the National Commission for Women, who felt the 'issue' needed 'widest consultation'.[19] The same body, in 2002, had reportedly argued for decriminalization of homosexuality during discussions on the Criminal Law Amendment Bill.

Those were the days when several sections of the press were starting to view us as legitimate beings. The salaciousness in reporting had reduced. It was also a time when we were far less visible in numbers, where mostly metro cities had Pride marches and weekly or biweekly gay nights at bars. At that point of history, there were hardly a handful of queer groups in universities or support communities online or elsewhere. Mental health wasn't much of a subject. When we spoke of suicides, we pinned the responsibility on the individual instead of the ecosystem being the disease, using the term 'committed suicide' rather than 'died of suicide'.

It was also a period when Bollywood portrayed us as

[19]'Govt Unlikely to Appeal HC's Gay Order on Its Own', *The Times of India*, 3 July 2009, https://tinyurl.com/yymbnkyd. Accessed on 25 September 2022.

caricatures, not characters, not that the truth of queer lives matters enough even today. And in the workplace, words like diversity and inclusion were not yet trending. We weren't worth a thought then, not even part of corporate social responsibility (CSR) initiatives or brand-building exercises that organizations could benefit off.

Notwithstanding these ground realities, we were hopeful that the order would stay. We didn't think it would be reversed in December 2013. We didn't think the Supreme Court would call us a 'miniscule minority'. We didn't imagine that the court would tell us to seek recourse from the legislature, choosing not to uphold the Constitution instead.

We knew that the Parliament was a hopeless body when it came to queer or women's rights, that political parties and politicians tended to buckle under pressure from religious groups, spiritual gurus, anyone who could guarantee them votes. We were aware that they were as much a part of society, representing a mindset that wanted to wish us away and keep women out of turfs that were 'made' for men. This meant, they'd rarely protect or speak for us or women, irrespective of the law (now) or the Constitution, usually using sanskriti or culture as excuses to put us in place.

When I first landed in the Thai capital, I assumed that the large presence of women in the local workforce and them roaming the city at leisure much past midnight, not once looking out of place, was a reflection of how safe the city was for them. My immediate thought then was that Bangkok's law and order, the system of policing, was doing its job. After all, in Delhi, it was the police that we usually blamed and claimed as the inherent problem every time a rape occurred on the streets of the city. It didn't occur to me that there was greater parity between women and men.

Thailand, I discovered, was largely a matriarchal society. Not that I was fan of power being wrested by one sex or the other, I didn't see an absolute control of women, the kind that the patriarch holds in most families in India. Yes, in several provinces, men moved into their wives' homes. Women mostly owned land. Inheritance automatically was for them to 'will' away. But, even if this sounds amusing, men weren't unsafe in their wives' homes or on the streets in cities, towns and villages. And matriarchy didn't turn women into rapists, in the way men had become in Delhi and other parts of India and the world.

Men worked too, just like women did. They had powerful roles in governance and businesses. For instance, the king ruled, not the queen. Men were monks, a highly revered group of people. And with globalization and the import of western gender equations generally favouring men, they had gone on to hold key positions in international corporations that had set up shop in the kingdom. Wives didn't 'deny' their husbands jobs. Men didn't need to seek their permission. Therefore, women didn't need to 'allow' their husbands to work and appear progressive and liberal.

There were other aspects about Thai society that appeared unique, as their kind of Buddhism saw marriage as a secular choice, not a duty or dharma. By the same token, a divorce was a choice too and was never a reason to stigmatize a woman or blame her for not having held on to the man, since a nuptial was always about two people, not one, not only the man. Marriages were also not about procreation. To have a child and when to have one was a choice.

At the core of Thai life, I learnt, was not just mai pen rai, it was about being and staying happy. My dear friend Nathanun Sriphyak, who is based in Bangkok and goes by the name Jaa, said the pursuit of happiness was very much personal yet sociocultural and religious too. 'It doesn't mean we have no duty towards our parents or children or carry no emotional bond,' she said. It wasn't any kind of selfishness or self-centredness either, it was more about centring the self, she explained, sort of distinguishing the popular mainstream idea of the 'I' and its consumeristic self-indulgence that is all-consuming and often always consuming.

Jaa, like many other Thai women, was at peace in her singlehood, her set of friends, the choices she had made and, as she said, 'the time I get with my son'. The mother–child equation, as it was in India, was special. But it wasn't obsessive in terms of attaching motherhood to a woman in a moralistic way, like it was their prime act, purpose or role in life. Therefore, the decision to have a child was the woman's. It was equal to their decision to have sex, a reassignment surgery, refuse any kind of intimacy and be queer or straight. And while men weren't denied these options, except, as it were, to bear a child was beyond their biological capacity, people generally understood that sex was between the legs and sexuality was in the mind, the heart and that it was expansive. This is why the nation had a significant queer population and was known for its history of 'lady boys'.

Clearly, the social constructs in Thailand were different—imperfect but different. Some Bangkokians revealed that the laws to protect women were important but the 'effectiveness' and 'greatness' I accorded to the police force was too generous. The reason being Thais were culturally aligned with the legalities, which only a few would test and break.

If I am to apply and explain this in an Indian context, I guess, one example is corruption. If to cheat the system and people and to be corrupt was and is culturally accepted, no law can be an effective deterrent. Similarly, if women were and are considered to be the lesser being, then the act of subjugation, the violence against them, is acceptable. No legality can curb inequality sufficiently or even halfway. Not when the enforcers themselves are part of families and communities that obfuscate the law, believing that their homes and the defined gender roles they follow are correct.

Therefore, in April 2015, when the Minister of State for Home Affairs Haribhai Parathibhai Chaudhary told the Parliament in a written reply that 'the concept of marital rape, as understood internationally, cannot be suitably applied in the Indian context,'[20] he was speaking for a large number of Indians and would appear justified in doing so. While he blamed poverty, and the level of education and illiteracy amongst the reasons for saying what he did, he stated that 'myriad social

[20]'India Not to Criminalise Marital Rape', *The Hindu*, 29 April 2015, https://tinyurl.com/2hwxz4u8. Accessed on 25 September 2022.

customs and values, religious beliefs', had to be considered, since marriage was a 'sacrament'. Meaning the male offender had to be excused, let off the hook or allowed 'to be a man', as this was what men were. And women were to accept this—that the sacredness of marriage provides the man with these allowances, a lifetime guarantee of patriarchy!

In our home, however, as you'd guess, roles were not cast in stone, and power as such was based on respecting the adults in a home and each other, even as we spoke our mind. But that wasn't necessarily the approach carried by many families we knew then or now.

When we moved to Delhi, my brothers and I took on duties, sharing the functioning of our first-floor residence. Duji looked after the paperwork involving banks, investments and taxation. Dipu, the most social of us three, helped with shopping and anything that gave him a reason to step out of home. I, as it were, preferred to help prepare meals and occasionally tend to Ma's growing collection of plants. As we couldn't afford more than one servant, a person who looked after the 'top-work', my brothers and I would split the job of laying the table and clearing it after a meal, washing and drying utensils, cutlery and crockery, and then placing them in their respective drawers and shelves.

Relatives and friends admired our family's resilience and ability to come together and share housework, what they saw as a consequence of economic compulsions, and therefore, a momentary exercise. Some of them thought Ma was downcast, telling her not to worry, 'The boys will soon be earning well, and their wives will be there to run the home and keep you company.'

Ma, however, wasn't downcast and had no such supposition. She was of the opinion that we all needed some 'home' skills, what is now commonly called 'life skills'. She saw it as a means of self-sufficiency and survival. 'It is a responsibility to the self, to a partner and for a couple and to their family,' she explained, emphasizing the point 'nothing is one person's job'. Years later, I asked her had there been a girl in our family, a sister to my brothers and I, would things have been different, for example, would she be relegated to the kitchen or the washing of clothes and serving guests. 'Why, what difference?' she replied quickly, offended by the question and that I had thought of such a marked difference between girls and boys.

If I were to take her response and apply it to today's discourse on the gendering of roles, she was surely not an advocate of the same, not the way roles are typically separated as part of a social order. What she admits to, though, was her acceptance of the popular notion (an Americanism) of blue being the colour for boys and pink for girls. In that she never bought pink-coloured clothes for any of us and thought none of her sons would or should wear pink. She also believed that dolls and dollhouses were for girls. Attire was also gender-specific for her. The same applied to jewellery, a chain was permissible for men, but anything worn by women weren't for the male sex. She also carried a view on the gait of a man and a woman, but most of that came from her training in Bharatanatyam, a dance form that was generally women-oriented. Hence, she believed there was a certain grace attached to a lady's walk as opposed to a man's.

Other than that, she had always seen the two sexes as the 'opposite' sexes playing their roles in the act of intercourse. This notion, of course, as it had to, changed when she learnt about my gayness. With this learning, she realized clothes were unisex, so was the manner in which one walked and that jewellery was for all, much like how it was for Hindu gods and Buddha, all stunning pieces of art and craftsmanship.

Even though my mother's idea of masculinity and femininity wasn't as fluid as she or I see things from today's standpoint, the flexibility she showed had much to do with the kind of life she had had in school in Dehradun and college in Delhi in the 1940s and 1950s. She had played hockey and been a gymnast, one of the few in Dehradun then. She had been a gold medallist in Bharatanatyam at a time when being a dancer wasn't socially accepted, since dancing to an audience was what courtesans did, not girls from respectable families

'We weren't made to feel that girls were incapable of anything,' she said. As a result, she wasn't forced or compelled to learn cooking, a 'job' that women were expected to know in preparation for marriage. Her sister, Uma, and cousins would roam around Delhi quite freely, as there wasn't any fear or the need to be chaperoned to and from college or for their various sports activities. Those days were safer for women, and at no juncture were they made to feel subordinate to men, she recalled.

Today, while there is a growing emphasis on women's independence, there is also a growing concern for women's safety in several cities, particularly Delhi. Which is why, when I asked Ma if my fictional sister would be as free as my brothers and I when she'd step out of the home, her response was filled with uncertainty and questions: would it be okay for her to wear what she'd like and go out at night without any dread? Would she be as safe as my brothers and I were? And would she be safe with men?

When Ma read my book *Straight to Normal: My Life As A Gay Man* and found that I had been raped and physically assaulted on different occasions, she learnt that gay men were at risk too. When she was told of the violence inflicted on some of my trans women and queer femme friends, she verbalized something that should have bothered most of us: 'It appears, anyone who doesn't appear masculine is a soft target!'

Since then, whenever I stepped out of home and the clock struck 10:30 p.m., Ma would call me to check if I was okay. That I was often at the Gulmohar Park Club, only half a kilometre away, was not enough reason for her to feel assured of my safety. To be honest, if the gates next to our main road residence were closed and I had to walk a longer route, almost two kilometres, I had my inhibitions and fear, looking out for shadows of men or if anyone was following me. The slightest sound of footsteps would amplify my anxiety, which hasn't gone away yet.

The law, I know, can't resolve these personal and cultural realities, not completely. Yet, I also know, we can't ignore the import of the law and wait for a cultural and social shift to give us some sense of self and confidence. In the words of the senior lawyer Saurabh Kirpal, who identifies as gay, 'Perhaps one of the most fundamental ways in which the law shapes us is in how we identify ourselves. Wife, mother, employer, lover...each of these roles is not merely a societal construct but a societal construct backed by a complex set of legal rules. A whole ecosystem of laws and regulations governs the interactions we have in such positions, with each other and, inevitably, with ourselves.'

While he argued that our very sense of identity is shaped by the law, he provided an example of how the law changed the status of married women. 'To be a Hindu wife before 1956,' he said, 'meant that the husband could have other wives as well, and children from those wives. A woman's right to property and inheritance was heavily restricted; she was merely seen as chattel'. Such laws, he points out, 'not only determined the legal status of a woman but inevitably devalued her self-worth.'[21]

Most queer folks would relate to Saurabh's studied observations. The lack of self-worth is linked with our legal status. Our identity has a limited locus standi as the complexity of laws doesn't have space for us. Even today, we are second-rate citizens in our country. As a lawyer once told me, 'Only social capital can give you certain benefits.' This means you need to be privileged and have access to the system to come close to being equal and to exercise certain choices.

It was around a decade ago when I attended a discussion on 'our' existence and those of women somewhere in Shahpur Jat, in a bare room that perhaps provoked us to strip the facades

[21]Kirpal, Saurabh, *Sex and the Supreme Court: How the Law is Upholding the Dignity of the Indian Citizen*, Hachette India, 2020.

of society to its barest. We all sat cross-legged on durries, the good old way, not compelling a woman to 'sit like a lady' or a man to 'sit like a man'. The floor and the durries, of course, didn't distinguish one from the other, and sukhasana, the yogic word for this posture, wasn't gender-specific. I suppose this was an ideal place and way to address 'our' issues and rights.

Many voices that afternoon suggested a women–queer alliance be formed. The logic was this—the liberation of women and the queer community is a common threat to society, and the common challenge we share is society's patriarchal ways—male. 'His' fears lead to all kinds of phobias directed at both groups. In the case of queer folks, it is trans and homophobia. As for women, it is rape, gender roles and the protective Lakshman rekha that provide safety, ironically, from the people who draw these lines—men. It would never free them, but who'd say that.

If a woman chooses a career, she'll somehow appear to be a competitor to men, not one man. If she outshines a man, it would challenge his masculinity, his power and hurt his ego. If women reject men, it would be the rejection of their manliness or masculinity. How could she do that and how could he allow the same? If a lady decides to be single, that in itself is seen as a way of dismissing the relevance of men to women, to a family and, eventually, society. Who'd create (procreate) and carry forward the legacy of a family and the man's name? Again, if she finds a lover, another woman, that could be far worse; it is abnormal not to live with a man. A woman is supposed to dedicate her life to him. She can only be a sexually active, heterosexual woman.

Similarly, if men dismiss the idea of marrying a woman, people like me, choosing a same-sex partner instead, he'd be called (as I was) a 'sissy' and 'girly'. That he chooses a man, means he must be some kind of a woman, as only women can be with men, so he must be half a man.

Just as some of us thought the discussion was over and there'd be a recap, someone shouted out, 'Let us not blame the man alone, women are also guilty of perpetuating stereotypes!' Mothers, as was pointed out, forgive their sons, and wives pardon them saying, '*Ye to hota hain, mard aise hi hote hain* (This is how it is, men are like this).' Being on his side means they can be part of that strength, force and the economics running on him. The mothers hope that they'll be looked after in their old age and the wife hopes for lifetime security for herself and her children.

No wonder then, a 2022 national survey by the Union Ministry of Health and Family Welfare found that 45 per cent of women were in favour of men assaulting their wives if they refused to 'perform her duties'.[22] No wonder, then, parents don't like to see their son cry or accept his emotions, which appears soft or feminine. They need him to be a man, the bread-earner and provider. And to keep that equilibrium, the woman has to be a woman—dainty, soft, submissive and feminine. Any deviation, therefore, has to be disciplined, leading to phobias turning into hate, the ones we talked about at the start of the meeting.

---

[22]Madhukalya, Amrita, 'Nearly Half of Indian Men, Women Think Domestic Violence Is "Fine" If Wife Doesn't Perform Her "Duties"', *Deccan Herald*, 9 May 2022, https://tinyurl.com/2cjxrjt3. Accessed on 25 September 2022.

Even without the data from 2022 and earlier years, I wondered, as did some others, if a tight and strong alliance between women and queer folks was a possibility. Would we have numbers backing such a proposition? Or would there be silent support; after all, for women and queer folks, coming out to share a secret, the pains they have lived with, is never easy.

Still, we left the bare room in Shahpur Jat hopeful, with a purpose and learnings from each other. A bunch of us—gay, lesbian and queer femme folks—walked towards the bus stop next to my residence close by. We were so charged up and absorbed by our discussion, we spotted gender roles playing out at every step we took towards our destination.

We stopped at a makeshift street-side vegetable store, as I had to buy some lemons, chillies and coriander. As my friends helped with the selection, we saw a woman carrying a child in one hand close to her chest, in the other, she held a heavy bag of what seemed to have been pulses, wheat and rice. The man beside her, who we gathered was her husband, given the way she addressed him, paid for the tomatoes she had picked. His hands were free. But he didn't think it necessary to help reduce the load she was carrying. Even when she requested him for help, he placed the tomatoes precariously at the top of the already heavy bag. We may have generalized that moment, but this was what typically defined male entitlement. He was evidently the bread-earner, and she was the lady providing the service (unpaid labour) of being a mother, doubling up as the person in charge of the kitchen and the rest of the home.

We saw advertisements reaffirming these roles, the only

difference was the product and its target audience, presumably from a higher economic stratum of society. One ad showed a lady selling a washing machine, most likely to other women who were to do the same task in their homes. Another, pasted in multiples on the wall partitioning the Asian Games Village from Shahpur Jat, had a lady claiming that the detergent bar she endorsed was 'new' and 'improved', implying the detergent bar was evolving but not the role of the woman. The third one we saw was of a mother with two children, suggesting that the specific soap she used protected her children from germs, that everyone else, meaning other mothers, should be as responsible as her and buy like her. As you'd guess, the woman was in charge of her children's health, the home and the family. Not the man.

According to my dear friend, noted historian Saleem Kidwai, there are always social, moral and legal aspects that creates a normal 'for the better or for worse'. However, normalization of anything, he explained, is heavily reliant on the simple Hindi adage '*Jo dikta hain woh bikta hain*'. In English, it loosely means what you see is what sells. It also means visibility sells. The ultimate meaning of the sentence, though, is this: what is most visible seeps into a person's consciousness. That consciousness, as it were, normalizes what it repeatedly reads, sees, views and experiences.

So, for example, if we are always shown Christmas as white, with snow and are told stories verbally and pictorially of Santa Clause on a sledge, heading down a hill, we'd never imagine the festival in hot and sunny regions of the world. That means we exclude how Christmas is celebrated in over 44 countries and more than a dozen others, where it snows rarely and only at 1,000 metres above sea level.

If the media repeatedly tells us that political parties 'come to power' and not to office as elected representatives of the people, we grow to believe they are power and rarely are conscious of the fact that we have empowered them. If we are told what is big, great, greatest, successful, happening and the most brilliant through every medium and influence, anything and everything else becomes largely irrelevant, probably invisibilized into obscurity.

By the same token, the kinds of ads that we saw in Shahpur Jat echoed and normalized a gender stereotype, according the woman motherhood only, denying her womanhood, the possibility of self-actualization. They were placing her in the eye of the man, not an image of herself by herself. Similarly, as the Nigerian author Chimamanda Ngozi Adichie observed, if only men were seen as CEOs and chairmen of companies, 'it starts to seem "natural" that only men should be heads of corporations.'[23] If we find boys being appointed as class monitors in schools, we'd never think of a girl in that role. As a result, given the long history gone into establishing these gender roles, most people, women included, would never think they have any other role to play.

On one of the evenings at Saleem's home in Delhi, at an adda of sorts, he said that to include and exclude is about

---

[23]Ngozi Adichie, Chimamanda, *We Should All Be Feminists*, HarperCollins Publishers, UK, 2014.

power structures defined and controlled by men to retain their position at the top. 'How many stories do we have of women, when they account for almost half of India's population and more than half the world's people?' Without those stories, who'd think they had a significant role to play in the past globally and in the subcontinent? Although women weren't always treated equally, 'Didn't their absence from history reduce the scope and imagination of what women were, can be; their strength to endure pain and come out triumphant, aren't these stories important for the future (generations) to learn and be inspired by?' he asked.

This is when he referred to his passion project, *Same-Sex Love in India*, the book Ruth Vanita and he put together. The book was part of the evidence produced in the Supreme Court seeking the reading down of Section 377. While he admitted that there wasn't enough evidence on the social status of queer people, 'we had enough material to show that we were there.' He talked about queerness in Vyasa's Mahabharata, the Panchatantra, the Puranas and the Kama Sutra. He spoke about the Persian–Urdu period and various poets and writers from different times—Amir Khusro, Muhammad Akram, Mir Taqi Mir, to name a few—who established variants within sexuality, proving that not everything was socialized the way it was.

'Alas, this history was reduced, blurred and overtaken by Victorian culture, laws and writers, mostly men, wearing the male heterosexual lens,' he said. As a consequence, we were left with a western import called homophobia, which 'may take eons to neutralize,' he lamented. And, 'we don't have enough muscle to counter the system.'

It was then that Saleem trained his eyes on me to say the following: 'Sharif, I hope you can get over your fears soon. We need your network to speak for us. We need more people like you out there.' He urged me to forget the homophobic campaign aimed at dislodging me from the post of CEO at Integral PR. He felt a lot of time had lapsed since my Hotmail account had been hacked and my gayness outed when I had still been a journalist. He felt it shouldn't matter if my drooping hands were mocked at by friends I played cricket with.

As I felt a bit cornered and, I think, he noticed it, Saleem smiled and said, 'Your time will come and you will know when.' He seemed to then invoke Harvey Milk when he said, 'We need more people out there and across the spectrum, a groundswell of queerness, a revolution of sorts'. But knowing full well that the subcontinent had never seen a nationwide 'collective' uprising, movement or revolt in its history, queer or otherwise, the charge in his voice and the excitement of challenging norms lasted only a few moments.

We tried to break the moroseness of our lived realities, chatting and laughing about Nirupa Roy's quintessential role as the mother searching for her sons (not daughters), the heroes, praying at temples for their health, safety and return. Even though it was a diversion, it was also a reminder of how difficult it is to shake off and erase those normalized images closely linked to societal stereotypes.

TWELVE

THE FIX

When I took the stage at Hard Rock Café, Delhi, in December 2013, I finally started to do what Saleem felt necessary for myself and indirectly our community—queering, to some extent, a very heterosexual space those days, the indie music scene. It was a tiny step and was days after the Supreme Court recriminalized homosexuality, an evening where my band, Friends of Linger, released 'Head Held High', a dedication to the LGBTQIA+ community.

Thanks to a near-full-page write-up in *HT City* and the anger against the verdict of the apex court, we had over 200 people in front of us, singing along to the chorus of the track. I don't know what came over me, but for the first time, I spoke publicly against the homophobic view of the court. I was critical of religious groups that supported the order and quipped about yoga gurus who were 'so flexible' they put their feet in their mouths while speaking about homosexuality, claiming they could cure us. I spoke about gayness and even explained where the word 'linger' came from, that it was to do with the ling, the puling and striling, and everything in between and besides.

I recall some people telling me to hold back, that I was a CEO, a professional. 'Yeah, but CEOs can be gay, they ought to get it,' I retorted.

Over the previous few years, I had grown in stature as a communications consultant. A few months prior to the gig, I had been named 'PR Person of the Year' at the India PR & Corporate Communications Awards (IPRCCA) and was in the midst of my second term as the president of the industry association, Public Relations Consultants Association of India (PRCAI). I was representing India on the board of the largest communications body in the world—International Communications Consultancy Organisation (ICCO)—and had already held a similar position on the global Public Relations Organisation International (PROI) board. And the consultancy I ran was winning awards, year after year.

For most people, every pat on the back are motivations to achieve more, believing the sky is the limit. But for me, and many like me, it is all about validation. Even if today I harp on the need to ignore '*Log kya kahenge* (what will people say)', it was the recognition in the eyes of the public, all strangers, and the media that made me believe I was good enough and equal enough. It was a way to tell myself that I was 'included'. That my sexuality was 'no longer' a hinderance, no reason to feel less or to go back into the closet.

As Saleem would say, visibility and presence could become references and inspirations for the gay community. They could inspire others to believe that even they could take similar steps, that they could be included too.

For generations, our references had mostly been western. But when Ashok Row Kavi came out publicly, we had an Indian gay man in the open. When Onir made films in Bollywood, we learnt that gay men could make films, good ones. When Ritu Dalmia said she was lesbian, we realized lesbians could turn out to be amongst the most-respected chefs in the country. When Satya Nagpal said he was a trans man, we knew that a trans man could be a national-award winning cinematographer. When Manabi Bandhyopadhyay was appointed a college principal, we learnt that a trans woman could be a principal and educator. When Saurabh Kirpal came out as gay, we learnt gay men could be senior advocates of the Supreme Court (and if all goes well, he could be the first gay judge of a high court).

Who'd think that trans women like to dance, that Abhina Aher, an activist and former sex worker would put together a transgender troupe called Dancing Queens? Who'd believe that transgender dancer Manjamma Jogathi's contribution to folk dance would be recognized with a Padma Shri? No one thought that lesbians could be athletes, until Dutee Chand came out. Who'd expect that a trans woman could be a screenwriter, like Gazal Dhaliwal. Or that a trans woman would head a Covid centre like Dr Aqsa Shaikh did, who is also an associate professor at the Hamdard Institute of Medical Sciences.

Of course, when Ruth and Saleem gave us *Same Sex Love in India*, we also learnt that queer folks can be stellar historians, that they did what other historians hadn't. Through their tireless research, we were made aware that the subcontinent has had a long queer history, one that had its own diversity. The fact is, queer folks come in different shapes, sizes, colour, skills and qualifications. They come with different lived experiences and intersections that either afford them greater opportunities or add to their struggles for survival. For example, when I listen to Dhrubo Jyoti, Dhiren Borisa or Jyotsna Siddharth, I learn how they are two times a minority being Dalit and queer too. But I see Dhrubo as one of the most admirable writers I've known along with being a senior editor. I find Jyotsna's strength in voice and filmmaking, exceptional. And Dhiren is an incredible intellectual, holding a doctorate in *Queer Cartographies of Desires*, a poet and assistant professor with the Jindal Law School.

There are many stories of grit and success across the country, of disabled queer people, of queer Christians and Muslims, of Adivasis, of lost childhoods, victims of violence, including rape and shock therapy aimed at converting a person to straightness. Some are heard and documented, some aren't, since survival, recognition and visibility, as such, all come down to opportunities of being seen and heard, to whether you can get your foot in the door. Or whether the door is open enough to allow what PM Narendra Modi has promised—*Sabka Saath, Sabka Vikaas*.

It was in November 2018, at a conference on diversity

and inclusion held in Mumbai, where Apurva Asrani, the 'out' national award-winning film scriptwriter and editor, said, 'Success seems to be the antidote to homophobia.' He believed that to 'do well' in the eyes of society is a way to neutralize hate against sexual minorities such as us. He took his own experience as an example: how his parents had accepted him when he won a national award in 1999, for editing the path-breaking film *Satya*. His home was filled with bouquets of flowers, celebrating and acknowledging his achievement. His mother and father received multiple phone calls congratulating them and praising the success of their son.

According to Apurva, his parents realized his sexuality wasn't a shortcoming. He was capable, meaning he was as 'good' as everyone else, and heterosexuals had 'accepted' their son. To him, as it is for most of us, having family with you is a strength and a reassurance. You could run to them whenever required. You wouldn't have to hide your pain or hold back on sharing who you love or talking about the life you lead. And when family is with you, no one else matters.

Given how circumstances differ from person to person, the need for employment differs within the community and is largely in contrast with the heterosexual world. For many a queer individual, jobs aren't only about validation or countering hate against the community or about income, expenses and supporting a household budget. It is also about privacy, as it helps them escape homo- and transphobic parents and relatives, giving them the financial means to have a shelter of their own in cities and towns far away. It is also about those who are thrown out of their homes, left on the streets to fend for themselves. Even a tiny one-room space is enough to feel free, to be oneself.

To ones who earn a bit more than making ends meet, the extra monies help them 'appear' equal, by living like others and consuming like them with the hope that their sexuality remains hidden behind their careers and lifestyles. And like me, perhaps, once the threshold of success is crossed, and a feeling of being included takes over, they may choose to be more visible and vocal.

But not everyone has the opportunities that Apurva and people of my background have. Speaking for myself, I had a number of advantages that gave me access to employment. I spoke English, a language that gave me an edge. I was educated and I had a class to reckon with. I had a network. I could take risks if I wished to, having a roof over my head and family support. Without these pluses, I would never have been able to show my skills, explore my talent or work hard. I would never have had the success and recognition that came to me, that allows me the freedom I have now.

During an offstage chat at the conference, we agreed that no one should feel compelled to prove themselves to be accepted. Why is commerce the solution when dignity and basic rights have nothing to do with financial capital or employment?

Our co-panellist, Rudrani Chettri, a trans woman, activist, model and actor, was plain honest, saying she may never have gone past the entry gate of the hotel we were at on any other day. If she did, the next barrier would have been a troublesome 'check' at the main door of the hotel. The security check, she pointed out, would not be about the security of the hotel and its guests, it would be about gender, social morality and whether she fitted in with cis-heterosexual people and whether she had the wealth and status to enter such a luxurious hotel. What she meant was that the power and stature of the invitation was her pass to get in, without which, she didn't fit in.

Rudrani, who went on to star alongside Neena Gupta in *The Last Colour*, a film that was longlisted for an Oscar in the Best Picture category, revealed that even today, entering a shopping mall isn't as easy as merely walking through. There is an assumption, 'due to how we have been portrayed', she said, that transgender women don't have the right to shop, to eat or to consume anything 'others' do. When she and I went together to give a talk at an office of an MNC in Gurugram, which claimed to be inclusive and an ally to the community, she was stopped at the reception. It was only after a few calls and clarifications that Rudrani was allowed in. When she entered the office premises, there were quite a few people who stared at her as though she was an alien. 'How can I feel welcome?' she asked me quietly.

After we left that office, I walked towards the metro station, preferring the quicker and easier option back to Delhi. I took it for granted that she would pick the same mode of transport. But Rudrani didn't. She found metros unsafe for transwomen; taxis were safer. It was a choice she had to make irrespective of the cost or her income.

According to her, there was hope and hopelessness. Inclusion, she said, was a bit of myth, a one-day exercise, an occasional hour at an office, a symbolic gesture and rarely a genuine effort that was long-term. Even if several corporations had the right intent, they somehow didn't take out sufficient time to understand the lives of queer folks. They had no idea how many people lose homes, don't have money for food or education. 'With the kind of mental health problems we carry,' she pointed out, 'how can we perform at the same level as others?' For she, and so many others who didn't get close to the entry points or were made to feel like outsiders, believed that companies, by and large, lacked empathy, diminishing the value of the word rather than giving it weight.

'They are too big and we are too small,' she said, gently laughing off a stark reality, a remark that stayed with me, resonating with the discomfiture I had with power politics, and how it ruled every walk of life.

While I had a healthy salary, and like anyone else, wouldn't mind a little more money in the pocket or in the bank, I had grown to believe that it was best for the consultancy I led to remain mid-size or smaller rather than growing to being huge. There was something special about the intimacy and connection between people that, I felt, would be lost if we grew too big. Size meant scale. Scale meant overt systems, processes and templates that confined people's abilities to boxes, to filling in the blanks in sentences written by others. It would mean no time to know each other, just timesheets to measure work and equate it with money. It would be about bottom lines and numbers, where people are reduced to statistics generating those numbers.

To me, such systems kill heart, mind, soul and the

naturalness of instinct and creativity. They stunt individual growth, much like the aesthetics of control that is commonly visible in new-age gated apartment complexes, where trees are trimmed in a uniform manner, bushes are clipped so that one looks like the other, where every blade of grass is equal and cut to size, denying them the choice to bloom naturally. It is the denial of nature, of the diversity nature brings to life and is in no way empathetic.

In multiple ways, these aesthetics are boxes, manufactured socially and culturally, industrialized for us to fit in—having a shape, size and characterization. It is the 'sold' aesthetics of beauty and ugliness. It is in the aesthetics of the perfectly sized body and bodies to be shamed. It is the aesthetics of modern educational qualifications and their supremacy and the narratives of doubt over traditional wisdom. It is the aesthetics of strength and muscle and the depiction of what is weak. It is in the social hierarchies and the ladders to climb. It is about whether you are 'with it' and 'fitting in'.

All of this culminates into rigid definitions of development, success, perfection and merit, all that holds the powerful mainstream together. It is everything that gives a person access, stature, influence, and the might and muscle that Saleem spoke of. Which obviously means: anything that doesn't conform to these descriptives and definitions, doesn't 'fit in', isn't 'normal', is 'unusual' and a 'risk'.

When I was appointed the CEO of the consultancy, a quick transfer from one group company to another, as the previous head had quit, there were detractors, people who doubted my competence and my style of working. To them, I was a misfit, unconventional and a risk, everything that didn't conform to their imagination of what a CEO is. My attire (mentioned earlier) didn't fall within their expected and normalized image of professionalism and sophistication attached to a suit and tie culture. I also didn't appear to be a typically 'strong' man. I didn't have the educational qualifications as well. I had a bachelors in English, without honours and had no experience of running a business either.

I ran the firm by instinct. I preferred an open office, encouraging people to walk in and out as and when they required or felt like, which, I was told, was unlike a professional corporation. But I wanted the workplace to be like a news bureau, buzzing with colleagues speaking openly, sharing ideas, not seeing thresholds to rooms and cabins as barriers, that there is someone greater sitting inside.

In a few years, I changed the increment system, inverting the economic pyramid, giving greater attention to the base. Salary hikes in terms of percentages were mostly lower at the top and higher at the entry and middle levels, even if performance ratings were the same. I carried the view that leaders don't exist without a team or a following, that the team mattered greatly, that for strategies to move from paper to action, we need people on the ground. When I look back, however, I think it was one of many ways to reduce the wealth gap between the few at the top and the many at the middle and the base of the pyramid.

Around a year later, I set up a National Advisory Team. The purpose was two-pronged. First, to reduce the dominance of the headquarter over regions, encouraging a more federal way of functioning. Second, to bring in a more diverse, multicultural approach to strategies for national clients. I'd insist we shouldn't silence a voice and opinion, and to back my decision, I'd often point to the rising relevance of regional language press, how the Congress was losing ground with its Delhi-centric decision-making and the emphasis on a high command, and why coalition politics was taking centre stage.

When it came to hiring, we weren't averse to 'outsiders', people who weren't from PR or other fields of communications. As a result, we had employed former hotel lobby managers, a bank teller, a flight steward, documentary filmmakers, social workers and drop-outs from school and university. My emphasis was on the emotional quotient of a person, how a candidate viewed current politics, media, family and love. It was also about how they expressed themselves, whether they understood consumerism or had been consumed by it. I thought it helped us suss out the candidates' level of care towards themselves and others, whether they were inherently empathetic or not.

Undoubtedly, not all of our assessments of people were accurate, but by and large, we had built an organization that was well-knit and had a heart. In fact, I pretty much knew everyone's idiosyncrasies, taste in food, anecdotes about their lives, their attractions, distractions and heartbreaks. One of the many outcomes was the joy I got in sending out personalized messages with every Diwali gift to some 100 odd folks in the company. I could write long emails on International Women's Day with particular stories on the lives of the women in our organization, acknowledging their gut and prowess.

Which is why, I am sure, when I completed a decade with the firm, I received handwritten notes from nearly every person across offices, pasted on a huge cartridge sheet, framed for posterity. The messages were affectionate, naughty, congratulatory, with some hoping to work together for another 10 years. I was overwhelmed. I had tears in my eyes when I unpacked this gift, which now hangs at the entry of my bedroom, a reminder of love.

I never imagined that doing small little things, just listening and talking, caring for each other, could lead to so much affection. I didn't think that removing the perpetual pressure of targets off individuals, sharing stories amongst a team, chipping in for each other's weaknesses, building on each other's strength, accepting so much sameness in the differences we had, could lead to such bonhomie.

On reading a 2016 report in the *Harvard Business Review*, I realized that our culture was inclusive. I also saw the freedom that we thrived on was amongst the reasons we did well, grew rapidly, notching, at one point, over 35 per cent growth. The report says, 'In analyzing three decades' worth of data from more than 800 U.S. firms,' it was found 'that companies get better results when they ease up on the control tactics.'[24]

I had quit the corporate world before Section 377 was read down. Maybe, as some of my gay friends said, the firm

---

[24]Dobbin, Frank and Alexendra Kalev, 'Why Diversity Programs Fail and What Works Better', *Harvard Business Review,* July–August 2016, https://tinyurl.com/2k2ex9dx. Accessed on 25 September 2022.

would have been extremely attractive to queer folks and other minorities, but I thought that was conjecture. In today's world, the emphasis is on size, might, success, wealth creation and so on. We'd need thousands and thousands of small firms for us to be included; we'd need a great deal of queer enterprise and leadership.

In January 2019, at my book launch in Delhi, Anand Grover, the lawyer who led the Naz Foundation's petition against Section 377, said we were at a stage to start neutralizing queerphobia. Since we were no longer criminals, we could petition the courts for equal rights. While he talked about the legal process, he felt that any person from the community who had the privilege to move the courts should be fair to everyone while prioritizing a legal battle. This meant, if there is a pecking order in society (that we live with intersections of caste, religion and disabilities), we must consider who is most abused and hurt as the primary subgroup to protect. Our first steps, therefore, should be towards protecting and strengthening the most disenfranchised. I thought his recommendation or philosophy of inclusion was applicable to just about everything.

If we look at the workplace and the imperativeness of having a job, organizations must assess each applicant beyond their qualification, language, accent and all the boxes that are normally ticked. Moulee C, the co-founder of Queer Chennai Chronicles, says, 'The typical corporate approach to inclusion is limiting as it does not acknowledge the intersectional identity challenges and struggles from queerphobia to trans trauma, or how caste minorities amongst the gender and sexual minorities may find it further difficult to navigate workplace dynamics.'[25]

Similarly, my friend, inclusion advocate and author of *Queeristan*, Parmesh Shahani, who has talked about the business case for LGBTQIA+ inclusion, has insisted that the filters used in selecting candidates for a job have to change. Meaning, the idea of merit can't be applicable in a deeply unequal system and society.

To push this point home, however, has never been easy. So many of us knew it isn't enough to hold conferences, create working groups in chambers of commerce or write an article here or there. In fact, at a few queer group meetings that I attended, the media often came into focus. There was optimism about the press running campaigns for us, if not creating a debate on rules and regulations. I was hopeful, like so many others, but not fully convinced of how much support we'd get from the press, be it about quality, consistency or representation.

When I started out in journalism, I was told the press was expected to be free, liberal and open. It was the journalists job to make governments and political parties accountable, checking the powers that be, including industry. Its role was to keep people informed on what matters to them, their daily lives, their rights, ensuring there is some sort of equality in society. We were to have at least two sides to a news report, which was to be dry and factual, not peppered with adjectives and emotions that bias publics one way or the other.

[25] Banerjee, Sanhati, 'Pride Beyond June: Decoding Mental Health Dynamics for Inclusive Workplaces', YourStory, 8 July 2022, https://tinyurl.com/t5593rrm. Accessed on 25 September 2022.

It was for all these reasons that the press was and is called the Fourth Estate or Pillar of democracy, a reason for most minorities to hope they'd be represented, finding a space in the consciousness of the people, the executive, legislature and judiciary.

However, once the Indian economy opened up and the media expanded in the years to come (and television, in particular, exploded), it became part of a marketplace. Newspapers, magazines, television and digital platforms turned into brands and products, running like any other corporation. I recall receiving letters from television channels saying they broke a story two or three seconds before their competition, suggesting they were better than their competitor. There were newspapers reducing their price, comparing the cost to a samosa. There were television channels talking about trust, some about reach and some about their connection with certain age groups or being the leader at prime time.

Therefore, in such a cut-throat market, it was inevitable for most of the press to shed some of its responsibilities as a pillar of democracy and a service to its people, to focus more on what makes money, what they can profit from.

From what I remember, between three and five years into India's much-famed reform process, we saw the demise of pages and sections in the mainstream press devoted to arts, crafts, folklore and music. The reason was the lack of scale and economics, and the inability of individual artists and communities to advertise in those sections. Effectively, art, which is an extension of a person or community, an expression of a thought and vision free of society's trappings, and could say so much or influence people in a soft and gentle manner, was knocked out.

To some, it didn't matter, but to others, it was the ominous sign of the times to come, of commercial interests taking over pretty much everything.

For example, once the economy grew and reforms seemed more settled, and when Bollywood got its industry status, Hindi films saw a significant change. We lost stories of the *Amar, Akbar, Anthony* genre. The qawwali disappeared. There was a diminishing number of scripts that engaged with the lives of the poor and marginalized. There was a push towards opulence—grand marriages, wealth and lifestyles of the upwardly mobile. According to my friend, journalist and author Avijit Ghosh, this occurred simultaneously with the rise of multiplexes, which necessitated the separation of people based on price points. While earlier, 'cinema was of the people', classified at most by certifications—Adult, Universal or U/A—the segmentation was now more about class.

What he meant was that in the past, people mingled in the old-style halls, whether they sat in the stalls or dress circle. There was some form of connection and commonness. But with class stratification, the market focussed on where the money was, the multiplex-goers, who'd not just pay more but also consume popcorn and coke, adding to profits. So, films were produced keeping in mind this paying audience, and not the disenfranchised, as there was no money running on them or their struggles for human rights.

Let me provide you with a more specific and researched account of how things have been changing. During the Lakme Fashion Week, 2006, when many a pen was busy recording every costume ruche and ramp twirl, P. Sainath was doing a head count, 'While the Lakme Fashion Week was on, farmers were committing suicide in Vidarbha, Maharashtra, to the tune of seven a day. Yet, there were all of six journalists covering Vidarbha in the mainstream press, while there were 512 covering the Fashion Week. The theme of the Fashion Week was cotton; yet within that time frame, nearly 50 cotton farmers killed themselves.'[26]

But who'd care of the farmer's health in any case? Suicides, as it were, mattered only if the rich or celebrated ended their lives. Mental health was only spoken about if a filmstar or some 'well-heeled' person talked about it, saying they are depressed, struggling through a harsh time. They'd be called brave for sharing their pain, while no one listened to the plight of the farmer or of the many queer kids who lost their lives, most recently (February 2022) being Arvey Malhotra, suffering at the hands of bullies and, reportedly, a biased school system that just didn't wish to listen to his complaints.

It wasn't a surprise, therefore, that the press has been equating hard work largely with 'burning the midnight oil' and not the tilling of the land or the drudgery that a domestic help is put through. It is about the hard work of an Indra Nooyi and not of the many women who walk miles to collect water and

---

[26]'Stories Behind the Story', *The Indian Express* Archive, 19 April 2009, https://tinyurl.com/3kpzf2d3. Accessed on 25 September 2022.

return home to feed a family and play the role of a mother to her children. And this skewed representation, over a period of time, has led to the notion and belief that we should incentivize the rich with more money while denying any reasonable lifeline of cash or resources to the poor, saying they'd lose incentive.

Therefore, most policymaking, opportunities to learn and earn, cater more and more to the haves, the people who were visible, have a voice and a palatable story. Not 'others', people who are invisibilized or have a limited presence, including us!

Of course, the shameful wealth gap in India is a by-product of this system of merit and exclusion. An Oxfam report says, 10 per cent of the population holds 77 per cent of the total national wealth.[27] Now, tie this in with data on representation in the press. When around 80 per cent of the population falls under Scheduled Caste, Scheduled Tribe and Other Backward Classes, the rest, commonly described as the upper castes, hold 106 out of 121 newsroom leadership positions, says another report from the same organization.[28]

Hence, inclusion has been and is bound to be governed by their limited idea of struggles. It is about a small section of the community. It is bound to be largely English-speaking folks from a certain class. It is about the elite. It is about the rich, all glamour and gloss and mostly urban representation. It

---

[27]'India: Extreme Inequality in Numbers', Oxfam International, https://tinyurl.com/4u2m8dy7. Accessed on 25 September 2022.

[28]'Who Tells Our Stories Matters: Representation of Marginalised Caste Groups in Indian Newsrooms', Oxfam India, 2 August 2019, https://tinyurl.com/4jhuvfuj. Accessed on 25 September 2022.

is about wealth markers and education. It is about marriage, due to its industrialization and commerce. It is within their comfort zone of inclusion and merit, those they feel somewhat more comfortable to sit with. It was and is their definition of equality, which doesn't disrupt their structure or benchmarks of laws and status.

One of the most telling remarks that almost summed up how inclusion happens in the minds of many people in the mainstream was in a message I received from a senior journalist of an English daily in Lucknow as recent as February 2019. The person said, 'To immerse in society and office, one has to compromise that identity.' Meaning, don't bring your full self to work or don't be your full self anywhere in society. Don't wear what resonates with you. Don't be authentic. Meaning, we've to curtail being ourselves.

The journalist (who wants to write a book about queer 'success' stories) also said our sexuality should be 'flaunted at special get-togethers', sort of reducing our queerness perhaps to a Pride march. Maybe this scribe's mind is a lot like some corporations who'd rather see us in our authentic self only once in the year, during Pride Month.

But when we celebrate Independence Day, as a people or nation, do we limit independence to a day? Is the tricolour of no significance on any other day? When we honour our republic and its adoption of a constitution, is it a function of a solitary day? Do we orphan it the rest of the year?

Perhaps we've already orphaned it in meaning and action! Why else is it assumed that the Constitution of India has one sexuality—heterosexuals—when it is about the people of India? It doesn't explicitly exclude or include heterosexuals, homosexuals, transgender, asexual, bisexual, intersex and the rest who make up the rainbow.

I know, there'd be many who'd say that not all journalists are like this. Not all corporations behave this way, just like the contention 'not all men are rapists'. That not all men wish to assume power that a patriarch usually has and holds on to. Yes, I know this is true. But in the chase for equality and the pace of change for women, the World Economic Forum, in a 2022 report[29], predicts that it will take 132 years to attain gender parity—as long as that!

So, if women can't have their place under the sun, when they are more than 50 per cent of the world's population, shouldn't we be worried? Shouldn't we be seriously queering the debate? Shouldn't we be calling out the falsehoods of a male-dominated society, where the law that we wish to be included in carries mostly the male lens? That men continue to hold the most dominant positions across the spectrum of our democracy. That women are still to hold the mic, still to be free in thought, not just in expression, that many are yet to come into their own!

Adichie argues that gender itself is not an easy conversation to have, 'because thinking of changing the status quo is always uncomfortable.' When asked why she uses the word feminist and not 'a believer in human rights', she says that would be dishonest. 'To use the vague expression, human rights, is to

[29]World Economic Forum, *Global Gender Gap Report 2022*, https://tinyurl.com/45s3nhuz. Accessed on 25 September 2022.

deny the specific and particular problem of gender. It would be a way of pretending that it was not women who have, for centuries, been excluded. It would be a way of denying that the problem of gender targets women. That the problem was not about being human but specifically about being a female human.'[30]

As a community, I am quite certain, most of us would not want to lose the specificity of who we are or what we've been through to be ourselves. We would not want to be at the receiving end of white supremacists who prefer #alllivesmatter rather than #blacklivesmatter, as though Black lives have been equal. Yes, #loveislove but #queerloveislove too, and it definitely has more strength and is more diverse in expression than the commonly understood meaning confined to #loveislove.

The idea is not to be a victim or to live in victimhood. Victims of rape don't need to be treated as such for the rest of their lives. But to expect victims to live like everyone else, respond to a handshake or hug the same way isn't quite fair or reasonable. You wouldn't expect an abused child to see life and live it in the same manner as a child who has been loved and cared for. You'd need specific solutions to help them through so that they are independent and free to explore themselves fully.

Dr Aqsa Shaikh, much like Adichie, says equality, in the way it works, fails to recognize the problems of 'historical stigmatization, discrimination, ostracization, criminalization and pathalogization that a particular community has faced.' Equity,

---

[30]Ngozi Adichie, Chimamanda, *We Should All Be Feminists*, HarperCollins Publishers, UK, 2014.

however, acknowledges these factors, as much as it notes the advantages of others. It is more just, she says, as it tries to make and find adjustments that provide more accessible ways to equal opportunities, an observation that Parmesh made when he referred to the entry point filters for a job.

Of course, we need equality and can't avoid the nature of the press or the inequalities of wealth distribution, of caste dominance or other kinds of discrimination. We need those voices that the media picks too and the influence that comes with them. But if we have to be fair to ourselves, we shouldn't forget our history and where our strength came from.

The Stonewall Riots in New York City and the immediate rise up came from the most vulnerable and non-conforming individuals—minorities within the larger minority of the rainbow spectrum. It was in the voice and actions of Marsha P. Johnson, a Black American drag artist. It was Sylvia Rivera, a transgender born to a Puerto Rican father and Venezuelan mother. It was Stormé DeLarverie, known as a butch lesbian, whose mother was African-American and father was White.

Not to sound selfish, expecting the most disenfranchised in our society and the queer community to fight 'our' battle, it is evident that most of the upper class invariably believe they have lots to lose—the aesthetics of their life and the social capital they have. Still, and at the same time, if we expect men (the beneficiaries of patriarchy) to stand up for women, then we must expect 'our' most dominant and elite to do the same, passing the mic, allowing space for our diversity to bloom, just as nature naturally does.

There isn't one idea of success, just like there isn't one way to live or die. Bob Dylan said, 'A man is a success if he gets up in the morning and gets to bed at night, and in between he does what he wants to do.' Rudrani says, 'Success is in our hands,' that inclusion is also up to us and about us. It is in our solidarity at the time of a crisis, in shared experiences, the sameness we have, the multiculturalism we bring. It is about identity, independence and interdependence. It is about being in the crowd and being alone. Eventually, although this is much easier said than done, it is about the self. That even *Sabka Saath, Sabka Vikas* depends on *aatmanirbharta* (self-reliance).

EPILOGUE

You may ask what happened to my search for freedom, a gay life and love? After all, those were the reasons I had first flown out to Thailand and returned to that country more than two dozen times. You may, perhaps, even want to know if the 'Land of Smiles' is still my plan B, the nation to move to, to settle down in on my own or with one or multiple partners.

The fact is, the more I have gotten familiar with Thai culture and while I continue to adore that country, I have grown to want elements of Delhi and India wherever I'd choose to live. I would like to have my friends, family, the diversity of food and culture, the absurdity of our politics, the beauty and ridiculousness of our cinema, or that we can eat wheat as much as we consume rice and millets, wherever I go. At the same time, as I continue to reside in the NCR, I would want huge chunks of Thai culture here, be it the queer world, the presence of women in the day-to-day and their safety, the cuisine, the fruits and vegetables and the abundance of simplicity. Above all and in particular, I'd wish to import its mai pen rai approach to life.

Over the years, I have come to realize that just like human beings and nature, there are many dimensions to a nation and culture, that not everything is appealing or desired or that we are not completely objective or rational. That although everything is perfect, even hate can be perfected, just like tools are sharpened to their sharpest, a world where we can pick and choose freely isn't an infinite possibility, no matter where you are.

So, while all of us need freedom to make choices, to engage and disengage with different aspects of being, a culture, history, country, politic or government, I have understood that my search was not really about a place to be in or go to. It was about the ingredients that I believed could make an ideal world or a better one.

In multiple ways, my struggle to find love, heart and freedom, started and focussed on the outside, but headed towards a search for the self, the inner being, not a measured construct or form. It has been about what the writer and philosopher J. Krishnamurti said: that the process of understanding the 'inner self' was about 'understanding the world'.[31]

It has been about being aware that the world would be better if people could move freely rather than only goods and products, sharing lives, resources, wisdom, culture and ideas. That the acquisition of all things material often took us further

[31]'From Public Talk 1, Paris, 5 September 1961', jkrishnamurthy.org, https://tinyurl.com/bdju7r39. Accessed on 11 October 2022.

and further away from people, cultures, the diversity of heart and love. It was to comprehend the fact that everything globalized and nationalized in the name of 'one world' and 'one nation' is usually about scale, control and the homogeneity that is enforced through it.

Yet, I have learnt and experienced that in this same world, the feeling of hopelessness stems from the fact that hope exists. That the same applies to the feeling of lovelessness. That love exists and can come and go. It has been to recognize the fact that the world can change, that laws can be implemented to legalize our existence, that a Chennai High Court can favour banning conversion therapy, that queer live-ins can be protected, and the Supreme Court can one day observe and note that queer relationships constitute a family.

In these travails through life, places, people, time and cultures, I have realized that in actuality we are as naked as nature, if we drop the veneers, labels, tags and judgements. It has been about seeing the transparent and beautiful nature in ourselves, in myself, that none of us or I could or should be restricted by geographies, political boundaries, politics, laws, religions and rituals, anything that is external, that comes in the way of natural progression and growth.

So, my journey, so far, to get to where I am today has been about coming of age, as Saleem had defined it, about being fully established as a gay person, getting to a point of being uninhibited, not having to hide anything, no secret to hold on to, the kind that many queer folks are compelled to live with. It has been about freedom and the expression that comes from it, that I don't need to seek validation for my existence.

And, most importantly, that I understand myself better and the world I am part of, that learning, freedom and queering is a continuous process till as long as I am!

I'm done with lying
Am done with sighing
Done with complying
To the lies I tell

I'm done with storing
Done the baggage of mine
I'm done with trying
To live with the lies I tell

I'm done with mining
I'm done with flying
Collecting many miles
For the lies I tell

Will the honest be so
Will the past leave so
Will today be so
Is the reality true so

Or is it just what I see so

I'm done with crying
And my tears ain't drying
As I've been complying
With the lies I tell

I'm done with extending
Courtesies and just smiling
Not living just surviving
For the lies I tell

I'm done with my truth
I've put up with many hoods
The disenchantment school
Of the lies I tell

Will the honest be so
Will the past leave so
Will today be so
Is the reality true so

Or is it just what I see so

I know
I've got to fell the lies I tell

I wrote this poem in May 2016, standing in the midst of a shopping mall, in far-away Atlanta, keying in my mind and mood in the notes of my phone. It seemed to capture the shedding of the trappings, the life I had led, to get to where I reached when I started writing this book during the second wave of Covid, when all we needed were essentials.

ACKNOWLEDGEMENTS

This book is about a journey in life—of observations, experiences, of ups and downs, and my personal beliefs. It is about others who I have engaged with, listened to, met and absorbed through their writings. It is resultant of all of this, as much as those who have continued to be with me, have saved me from dying by suicide, pulled me out of depression or given me the intangible value of love.

My mother, of course, has been an incredible pillar of strength. Even during the past two years, when Covid struck the world, she never gave up on looking after me, although I tried to take charge of home, wanting to pay back for all her love and caring. She has patiently listened to my readings of some of the chapters and given her inputs too.

I wish my father was around to see where I have come in life, this book in particular. I am sure his genes are visible somewhere in this piece of work, and I am grateful for that. I am lucky for the clippings of his writing that we have retained as well as the books he wrote, a rich legacy left behind for us.

I am also grateful to my late brother, Duji, who opened my mind to everything about myself that I hadn't seen or known. He had and continues to inspire me. My eldest brother, Dilip, has egged me on during the process of writing, reassuring me of funds if this is the path I take—of being a writer—aware that this line of work doesn't necessarily pay well and my savings may eventually evaporate.

I remain indebted to Anjali Gopalan for being one of the most generous people I have known. Not only did she fight for us, her open mind and home, and warm heart, has healed me ever so often.

I have also been lucky to have the care and support from Allard Van Veen and his wife, Valerie, who made me comfortable in the PROI network. They were aware of my emotional fragility, holding my hand whenever needed. Clare Parson, belonging to the same network, was another strength, amongst the first people to encourage to find my voice through music, poetry and writing.

On my trips to Thailand, I always had the affection and time from Helmer Juul Nissen. He ensured I was never alone. But sadly and shockingly, he passed away in 2019, hours after we exchanged notes on our plans to meet in December that year.

During the course of penning my experiences and reflections, I had the good fortune of having freewheeling discussions with multiple people. Some of them with former colleagues, others with those who I met due to projects, conferences or common interests. And, of course, there are many friends and relatives too.

I was lucky to have had a friendship with the lovely and brilliant Saleem Kidwai, who was hoping to see the finished product. I had promised to deliver a signed copy in person, travelling to Lucknow to celebrate it over what he called the perfect marriage of mutton and alcohol, and pleasurable distractions such as gossip, poetry and memories. Alas, we lost him in August 2021, a loss that came quite suddenly.

I was blessed to get time from and with a few of my friends in the media. They include Avijit Ghosh, Jayanta Roy Chowdhury, Nandini Sengupta, T.K. Arun and Poonam Saxena. I have also been fortunate to have been able to pick the brains of the political commentator, analyst and author Dr Sanjaya Baru; adman, columnist and author Santosh Desai; and the London-based mythologist and storyteller Seema Anand.

I had long calls with the screenwriter Gazal Dhaliwal; Roy Wadia and his partner, Alan Hsuing; the grassroots queer feminist activist and author Maya Sharma; actor and model Rudrani Chettri; poet and medical practioner Dr Aqsa Shaikh; as well as the now-retired Wayne Waterson. I also had tête-à-têtes with the fashion accessories designer Akassh K. Aggarwal; the activist and founder of an online community group Indrajeet Ghorpade; the academic and teacher Sattrawut Bunruecha; the artist Mrinalini Singh; the poet Divesh Wadhawan; the marketing and sales professional, Nathanun Sriphyak; the co-founder of Nazariya: QFRG Rituparna Borah; and the editor of *Gaylaxy Magazine* Sukhdeep Singh.

I was also fortunate to get my masis—Pam Malhotra and Rama Dhawan—to go back in time to give me a sense of their younger years. I had similar conversations with my mausa, Harish Malhotra, who, unfortunately, is no longer with us.

Over the last few months, getting closer to the end, I managed to hold a few reading sessions with patient listeners, often over lunch and dinner at my favourite Gulmohar Park Club. This is when I got the attentive ears of friends, including Bhuwan Khaturia, John Oinam, Neelam Gupta, Vinod Kumar and Smruti Jalpur. I also had my aunt and uncle, Rita and Sudhir Kapoor; cousin, Sandeep Dikshit, with his wife, Mona; and cousin, Latika Dikshit, as an audience. And over the phone, late at night, I had my friend Rohit Sharma and cousin, Mehtab Malhotra, hearing me out.

When tired or restless, I could turn to Sujay Mehdudia, who'd calmly guide me through the moment, taking on the role of an older brother. I could call or walk in and out of my dearest friends M.K. Venu and Chitra's home, knowing that I would be cared for. I did the same with my childhood buddy, Nitin Mantri, and his wife, Rachna, with whom I'd chat late into the night. I also took much-needed breaks, entertained by my dear pal and 'bro' Vivek Mansukhani's humour and placidity, sometimes pulling him out of his home last minute.

There were occasions when I hit horrible lows but was kept afloat and away from depression by my chosen family of musicians hailing from different parts of India and the world. They have been a continuing reminder of hope, that their distinct personalities and specializations as indie musicians and the disparate instruments they play can come together to create harmonies and be harmonious. I am indebted to the Panamanian drummer and percussionist Fidel Dely Murillo; keyboardist and vocalist Guelor, who is originally from the Democratic Republic of Congo; the Delhi-based bassist Madhur Chaudhary; vocalist Parvati Krishnan from the tea gardens of Dibrugarh; and guitarist Shrikant Biswakarma from Siliguri.

I also found a great deal of respite and joy in the love of the very special Roshan Wosti. He has not just given me strength but has helped me look at life from different prisms, telling me, for instance, that a black cat crossing my path need not be bad luck but a premonition instead.

I have also been blessed with one of the finest people I know as my editor (and now friend), Dibakar Ghosh. He has helped me stay focussed, been a shoulder to lean on and an honest critic. He is someone who reads my mind and emotions, and hence, brings an incredible amount of ease to the process of writing.

I thank all of these wonderful people for the various roles they've played in the making of this book. I am eternally grateful for their love, kindness, intellect and brilliance.

Believe me, these words are not enough to express what I feel in terms of gratitude!